POWER
IN WEAKNESS

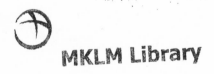

POWER
IN WEAKNESS

Second Corinthians
and the Ministry of Paul

Marty Wooten

One Merrill Street
Woburn, MA 01801
1-800-727-8273 FAX (617)937-3889

Power in Weakness

©1996 by Discipleship Publications International
One Merrill Street, Woburn, MA 01801

Printed in the United States of America

Cover design: Chris Costello
Interior layout: Chris Costello and Laura Root
Cover photograph: courtesy of Edmonson and Father, Photography

ISBN 1-884553-98-2

To my wife, Cathy, whose love for God and support of me have resulted in the writing of this book. May those who read it see not only the ministry of Paul, but her ministry as well.

Contents

Second Corinthians: Theology and Life

Introduction

Have you ever expended yourself for God and for others, only to find that the results were not what you expected? Have you ever been tempted to lose heart? Have you ever wondered if sacrifice and dying to self are really worth it? In 2 Corinthians the apostle Paul opens wide his heart to his Corinthian brothers and sisters and to us. He exposes his pain, shares his personal moments of despair, and allows us to enter the world of his own temptations. All of this vulnerability has a purpose: to show us how God works through tough times, how he uses our weaknesses for his purposes, and how in Christ there is always the hope of being prepared for the next challenge.

If you are trying to understand how your humanity and God's divinity work together to fulfill God's purpose of changing the world, then Paul's message in 2 Corinthians is one that God can use to transform your thinking and life. And if you care about having a deeper relationship with God and a greater reliance on him, read on!

Second Corinthians is one of the most important letters in the New Testament because it opens the door to Paul's heart and ministry like none other. Written by a man on the *field* of world missions—by one of the most prolific church-planters of the first century—it provides us with much needed insight into the perspective and emotions of personal ministry. It contains a wide range of information, including more in-depth theological material such as:

- the contrast between the written code and the ministry of the Spirit (3:1-6)
- the fading radiance of Moses (3:7-18)
- the treasure in jars of clay (4:7-12)
- the clothing of the mortal body with immortality (5:1-10).

But the letter also includes very practical texts, such as:

- experiencing the sentence of death (1:8-11)
- building trust in young disciples (1:18-22)
- being confident in the midst of persecution and suffering (4:8-12)
- sacrificial giving (chapters 8 and 9)
- living with a "thorn in the flesh" (12:1-10).

Paul's letter shows the important blend of the meat of God's word with its practical application to our lives and ministries.

Acts 15:39 through 18:22 serves as a record of Paul's second missionary journey, at which time he planted the church in the great Greek city of Corinth. The old city of Corinth was totally destroyed by an invading Roman army in 146 B.C. and stood in ruins until Julius Caesar had it rebuilt around 46-44 B.C. Caesar's decision was based on its strategic military and economic significance as an important stop between Rome and Ephesus and the rest of the cities on the Mediterranean and Aegean Seas.

Like progressive cities today, Corinth was full of different philosophies, religions and ideologies. Unlike Athens, Corinth never became known for its contribution to Greek culture or philosophy, but was known primarily as a vice-ridden city where morality was loose. All of this was mixed in with an atmosphere of religiosity, as Corinth was the center for the worship of the Greek goddess Aphrodite, the goddess of love and beauty. Sensuality and spirituality were seen as complementary and harmonious, and worshipping her involved immorality with temple prostitutes.

The depravity of the city obviously contributed greatly to many of the problems within the Corinthian church, such as the arrogance over possessing the spiritual gifts (1 Corinthians 12 and 14); the tolerance of immorality within the church (1 Corinthians 5); the ease with which the Corinthian Christians mixed participation in the Lord's supper with that of the pagan festivals (1 Corinthians 10:14-30); and the great impression they had of the false teachers whom Paul called the "super apostles" (2 Corinthians 11:5).

Purpose of the Letter

The primary purpose of 2 Corinthians was to rebuild the relationship between Paul and the Corinthians. It is obvious from reading 1 Corinthians that the church was young, immature and dealing with a variety of issues. Just as serious was the fact that their relationship with Paul was eroding. The contents of 1 Corinthians 4 show that the Corinthians, for whatever reason, had become arrogant in Paul's absence, developing an attitude that was unappreciative and independent of Paul. Paul warns them that, like children, they constantly need a relationship with their father. 1 Corinthians 9 indicates that the Corinthians had decided to financially support Paul no longer, which forced him to defend his right to earn a living from the fruits of the gospel. The problem obviously became so serious and sensitive that Paul decided not to exercise that right but to forego it and find support elsewhere.

The letter of 2 Corinthians provides more evidence about the influences behind the Corinthians' criticalness of Paul. Besides their own ingratitude and arrogance, the Corinthians were being influenced by false teachers, whom Paul refers to as "false apostles, deceitful workmen, masquerading as apostles of Christ" (11:13). Exactly who these teachers were is hard to know, but 2 Corinthians and some other New Testament references give us some indication. First of all, it appears that they were Jewish in background and were familiar with, or had even embraced, the teachings of Christianity, as Paul writes in 2 Corinthians 11:21b-23:

> What anyone else dares to boast about—I am speaking as a fool—I also dare to boast about. Are they Hebrews? So am I. Are they Israelites? So am I. Are they Abraham's descendants? So am I. Are they servants of Christ? (I am out of my mind to talk like this.) I am more.

Second, the false teachers were probably teaching some of the things that prompted the meeting in Jerusalem recorded in Acts 15:1-2:

> Some men came down from Judea to Antioch and were teaching the brothers: "Unless you are circumcised, according to the custom taught by Moses, you cannot be saved." This brought Paul and Barnabas into sharp dispute and debate with them. So Paul and Barnabas were appointed, along with some other believers, to go up to Jerusalem to see the apostles and elders about this question.

Paul also had to challenge this false teaching of salvation by Jewish works in the churches in Galatia, which prompted his letter to the church there. It is not hard to see Paul's deep convictions about this false doctrine in Galatians 1:6-9:

> *I am astonished that you are so quickly deserting the one
> who called you by the grace of Christ and are turning to a
> different gospel—which is really no gospel at all. Evidently
> some people are throwing you into confusion and are trying
> to pervert the gospel of Christ. But even if we or an angel
> from heaven should preach a gospel other than the one we
> preached to you, let him be eternally condemned! As we have
> already said, so now I say again: If anybody is preaching to
> you a gospel other than what you accepted, let him be eter-
> nally condemned!*

We know from later in the Galatian letter that Paul is
dealing with the same problem as we find in Acts 15:1-2.

> *Mark my words! I, Paul, tell you that if you let your-
> selves be circumcised, Christ will be of no value to you at
> all. Again I declare to every man who lets himself be cir-
> cumcised that he is obligated to obey the whole law. You
> who are trying to be justified by law have been alienated
> from Christ; you have fallen away from grace (Galatians
> 5:2-4).*

Though it is impossible to know for sure, Paul's contrast between the old and new covenants in 2 Corinthians
3:1-18, particularly his statement, "for the letter kills, but
the Spirit gives life" (3:6), is a good indication that the
doctrinal problem in Corinth was the same or very similar to the issue of circumcision mentioned above. Paul's
admonition in 11:4 is very close to what we saw in Galatians 1:6-9.

> *For if someone comes to you and preaches a Jesus other than
> the Jesus we preached, or if you receive a different spirit from
> the one you received, or a different gospel from the one you
> accepted, you put up with it easily enough (2 Corinthians 11:4).*

The issue of circumcision raised the whole question
of legalism—seeking God via "dos and don'ts" instead of
with heartfelt devotion and love—which is a root cause

of criticalness and division in the church. It is obvious that the Corinthians had become critical of Paul, as the Galatians had. Though we cannot be sure of all of the reasons why, legalism apparently had something, if not a great deal, to do with it.

To better prepare yourself to understand the issues in 2 Corinthians, take a few minutes to become familiar with the following chronology and the outline of 2 Corinthians. This will be time well spent.

Chronology of Events Between Paul and the Corinthians

1. Paul planted the church in Corinth (ca. 50 A.D.; Acts 18).
2. Shortly after planting the church, Paul was persecuted and forced to appear before Gallio, the proconsul of Achaia (ca. 50-51 A.D.; Acts 18:12-17).
3. Paul wrote a letter to the Corinthians, which we do not have today (1 Corinthians 5:9), and warned them not to associate with sexually immoral, greedy, swindling, idolatrous people who call themselves Christians.
4. The Corinthians wrote Paul back, seeking clarification about many of the issues discussed in 1 Corinthians 7 through 15 (1 Corinthians 7:1).
5. Some from Chloe's household informed Paul about the growing division in the church (1 Corinthians 1:11-12).
6. Paul wrote what we now call "1 Corinthians" to deal with the issues the Corinthians had raised in their letter and the problems that had been reported to him. He also stated that he was expecting to visit them soon (1 Corinthians 16:3-9).

7. Paul sent Timothy as his representative to remind the Corinthians of his way of life as a disciple (1 Corinthians 4:17). It is unclear exactly when Timothy was sent. It could be that he was the one bringing the letter of 1 Corinthians with him, or it could be that he was still en route when the letter was being written.

8. It appears from 2 Corinthians 2:1 that Paul had made a visit to the Corinthians sometime between the writing of 1 and 2 Corinthians. It is hard to know exactly when this "painful visit" took place. However, it did not seem to bring about the desired results.

9. Because of the deteriorating relationship with the Corinthians, Paul wrote still another letter (2 Corinthians 2:4; 7:8). This letter could be 2 Corinthians, or it could be another one altogether.

10. The Corinthians repented and had a change of heart (2 Corinthians 7:9-16).

11. Titus had also been sent to the Corinthians and was encouraged about their response to him (2 Corinthians 7:13b-16).

12. Paul wrote 2 Corinthians with the primary goal of re-establishing his relationship with the Corinthian church, to deal with the accusations of those who were undermining his apostleship (2 Corinthians 10); and to deal with the collection for the poor (2 Corinthians 8).

Outline of 2 Corinthians

1. Greetings to the Corinthians (1:1-2)
2. Paul's praise to God for comfort in affliction (1:3-11)
3. Paul's defense of his motives and integrity (1:12-2:4)
   a. The reason for his change in plans (1:15-2:3)
   b. His concern for the Corinthians (2:4)
4. Congregational reaffirmation of love for the sinner (2:5-11)

1

The God of All Comfort

2 Corinthians 1:1-22

As a leader, how do you start a letter to a church where you have your critics who are seeking to undermine your credibility? Do you list your accomplishments? Do you remind them of all the ways you have helped them in the past? Do you confront them about their arrogance? Paul did not do in this letter as many would have expected. After the normal introductory greetings, he does not hesitate to place a remarkable emphasis on his own infirmities and needs. He is most concerned to show from the very beginning that his confidence does not rest in himself but on God's power. He will defend himself and his decisions at certain points, but his emphasis clearly remains on the faithfulness and reliability of God and his own need as a disciple to rely on God's strength.

> *1:1Paul, an apostle of Christ Jesus by the will of God, and Timothy our brother,*
> *To the church of God in Corinth together with all the saints throughout Achaia: 2Grace and peace to you from God our Father and the Lord Jesus Christ.*

Though today we often refer to the letters of the New Testament as "books," many of them are, in fact, letters written to various individuals, churches or groups of churches. For example, we know that Paul wrote twice to the young evangelist, Timothy. These letters have become known to us as 1 and 2 Timothy. Often the author wrote to a single congregation, such as Paul's letter to the church in Rome, or to a group of churches, such as Peter's first letter: "To God's elect, strangers in the world scattered throughout Pontus, Galatia, Cappadocia, Asia and Bithynia" (1 Peter 1:1). Ancient letters, like our letters today, had certain characteristics. In the first century, letters usually began more like a modern memorandum with the author's name and the recipients mentioned first, followed by a short greeting or salutation.

The God of All Comfort

> [3]*Praise be to the God and Father of our Lord Jesus Christ, the Father of compassion and the God of all comfort,* [4]*who comforts us in all of our troubles, so that we can comfort those in any trouble with the comfort we ourselves have received from God.* [5]*For just as the sufferings of Christ flow over into our lives, so also through Christ our comfort overflows.*

Suffering and death are part of the world in which we live. Though in many nations of the world, technology has a way of shielding us from these realities or allowing us to hide from them, death is part of all of our destinies. The loss of loved ones and friends is a continual part of human existence. Disease and illness constantly remind us of the reality of the saying, "From dust we came and to dust we return" (see Ecclesiastes 3:20).

It is in this arena of human suffering that Paul presents God as the "God of all comfort." And though it is clear from the objective evidence of the world around us that everyone needs this comfort, the central point that Paul is making is that God becomes a God of comfort only to those who recognize this need. The difference between what is objectively true and what is personally recognized can be far removed. The world provides ample objective evidence of everyone's need for God. However, the need that Paul is addressing is the subjective or personal recognition for God. This recognition is born out of tribulation, suffering and, as in Paul's case, near-death experiences.

Though we can learn much about God from observing the world he created, the real specifics of God's character can be discovered and understood only because God has decided to reveal himself. This he has done through the Bible (2 Timothy 3:16), historical events such as the deliverance of the Israelites from Egyptian bondage, and most importantly through the life and death of his son, Jesus Christ. Hebrews 1:1-2 states,

> *In the past God spoke to our forefathers through the prophets at many times and in various ways, but in these last days he has spoken to us by his Son, whom he appointed heir of all things, and through whom he made the universe.*

And yet, there is still another way that God reveals himself to us—through the experiences in our lives. Without them our knowledge of God is greatly limited and remains abstract and impractical. Nearly every page of the Bible speaks about trials and sufferings and those who have lived victoriously through hard times: Abraham, Noah, Moses, Joshua, David, Ruth, Mary, Paul and of course, Jesus. God used intense times to humble these heroes in the faith and open their eyes so that they could see his nature more clearly. And God does the same for us today.

For example, God is able to reveal himself as a *saving* God only when we first humble ourselves and recognize that we are lost. God is a God of deliverance only when we admit our slavery. In the same way, God cannot be a God of comfort to us personally until we are first willing to carry our cross daily as disciples. Most people seek comfort by avoiding difficult circumstances. The disciple of Christ has decided not to run from challenges, so he or she must turn to God for the power to endure.

God is indeed a communicator and enjoys nothing more than showing us more and more of his nature. But until we are willing to embrace the challenging experiences through which God can be found, we will be like the Israelites whom Paul describes as having a veil over their minds and hearts when they read the old covenant (2 Corinthians 3:14-15). In this case, however, the teachings and promises of Christ remain a mystery to anyone failing to embrace the challenges to which God calls his disciples.

In this particular context (2 Corinthians 1:3-5), Paul shows the inseparable bond between suffering and comfort. Those who most powerfully experience the compassion of God and know him as "the God of all comfort" are those who meet him at the extremes of suffering. The Bible deals with suffering in a way completely different than the world. To the world suffering is a stumbling block that often confuses and disorients people, leaving most hopeless, despondent and bitter. However, to God suffering holds endless possibilities for spiritual growth. Peter says that suffering refines our faith (1 Peter 1:6-7). Paul rejoiced in his sufferings because "suffering produces perseverance; perseverance, character; and character, hope" (Romans 5:3-4). The writer of the book of Hebrews has a totally different slant on discipline and suffering than what we are accustomed to:

> *Endure hardship as discipline; God is treating you as sons. For what son is not disciplined by his father?...No discipline seems pleasant at the time, but painful. Later on, however, it produces a harvest of righteousness and peace for those who have been trained by it (Hebrews 12:7, 11).*

Although this concept is not totally absent in the world (we have all heard the saying, "No pain, no gain"), the important difference is that as a disciple, the rewards are eternal, but in the world the rewards are always temporal.

In Acts 9:16 God told Ananias of his plans for Paul's

life: "I will show him how much he must suffer for my name." It seems normal for most of us to think that God meant to punish Paul for persecuting the church. Imagine yourself being called into the ministry only to be told by God himself that you were going to be an example of suffering for the rest of your life. Most ministers today are given vision and encouragement by those training them and are told how great they are going to be and the incredible impact on the world they are going to have! Paul was given that vision:

> *"The God of our fathers has chosen you to know his will and to see the Righteous One and to hear words from his mouth. You will be his witness to all men of what you have seen and heard" (Acts 22:14-15).*

But he was also given a vision of intense personal suffering.

Our present passage (1:3-5) gives us insight into God's purposes for his statement to Ananias about Paul. One of the rewards of suffering is found in the ability it brings to minister to and comfort others. In other words, suffering or affliction is necessary to understand how to sympathize with the pain of others. Comfort is more meaningful from those who understand, and understanding follows suffering. Being comforted always finds its ultimate fulfillment in ministering to the needs of others.

> *[6]If we are distressed, it is for your comfort and salvation; if we are comforted, it is for your comfort, which produces in you patient endurance of the same sufferings we suffer. [7]And our hope for you is firm, because we know that just as you share in our sufferings, so also you share in our comfort.*

We must remember that this letter is not just a theological treatise but has a very practical and definite purpose. Paul is being criticized by the Corinthians primarily because of the influence of false teachers (see Introduction, page 15). Having had to change his plans to visit the Corinthians, Paul was being criticized as being fickle and undisciplined. However, Paul had faith that God was in control and that there was a purpose for his being retained in the province of Asia. He was confident that what he learned in Asia would in turn benefit the Corinthians: "It is for *your* comfort and salvation" (1:6, emphasis added).

Felt Like Dying

> *8We do not want you to be uninformed, brothers, about the hardships we suffered in the province of Asia. We were under great pressure, far beyond our ability to endure, so that we despaired even of life. 9Indeed, in our hearts we felt the sentence of death. But this happened that we might not rely on ourselves but on God, who raises the dead. 10He has delivered us from such a deadly peril, and he will deliver us. On him we have set our hope that he will continue to deliver us, 11as you help us by your prayers. Then many will give thanks on our behalf for the gracious favor granted us in answer to the prayers of many.*

Here we begin to see the reason why Paul was detained in Asia and was not able to return to the Corinthians—Paul and his missionary party were under great, and almost unbearable, pressure (1:8). Paul actually felt like he was looking into the face of death! The language Paul uses to describe the event is intense and indicative of the type of life-style God had called him to live. Yet, these verses are also filled with Paul's hope, deliverance and spiritual growth, which in fact give God's plan for intense suffering its vindication. God now emerges out of the dust of trial and suffering as "the God of all comfort" (1:3).

Unfortunately, it typically takes such extremes to teach us the basic fundamental truths about God and spiritual living. Our need for God is comparable to our physical need for air and water, yet understanding this is the most difficult spiritual lesson to master. Our flesh is in a constant state of attempting to rip us from the source of our creation and sustenance—our relationship with God. God helps us in restraining the flesh by showing us the futility and weakness of the flesh through the trials and sufferings of life. These experiences are intended to bring us to a conviction about what is truly important in this life.

Near-death experiences do not produce a conviction about needing to be more materialistic or selfish, nor do they provide the assurance that the flesh has immortal capabilities. On the contrary a more spiritual perspective of life and a gratitude for the simple necessities of life are usually the result. Successful spiritual living is achieved by a devotion and mastery of the fundamentals, such as faith, joy, contentment and reliance on God. This is what brings true spiritual contentment to our lives. Paul says in Philippians 4:11, "I have learned to be content whatever the circumstances." That learning process, as we have already seen, involved a consistent and regular exposure to suffering and trials for the sake of Christ.

God's Grace Not the World's Wisdom

> *[12]Now this is our boast: Our conscience testifies that we have conducted ourselves in the world, and especially in our relations with you, in the holiness and sincerity that are from God. We have done so not according to worldly wisdom but according to God's grace.*

In 1 Corinthians 1:18-2:16, Paul had spent considerable time comparing the wisdom of the world with the wisdom of God. It would be good to review this section in order to see why Paul was determined not to conform to the wisdom of the world. The reason Paul deals with wisdom is undoubtedly because of the influence worldly wisdom was having on the church in Corinth. The word "worldly" is the same word in Greek for "flesh" and con-

veys the absence of spiritual thinking when making decisions. Paul was letting the Corinthians know that he dealt
with them according to spiritual principles and God's
grace. There was no malice, impure motives or greed
when dealing with them, but rather, humility, gratitude,
servanthood and love. These were the spiritual qualities
that defined the heart of Paul and what the Corinthians
desperately needed to see in him.

Paul mentions the purity of his conscience in dealing
with the Corinthians and by so doing raises an important
issue in making spiritual decisions: How is it possible as
Jesus' disciples to always know God's will? Though the
Bible is our standard and provides all that we need for
living as disciples, there are many decisions that we must
make which are not specifically mentioned in the Bible:
*Where should I go to college? Should I try to change jobs
and make more money? What kind of car should I drive?
Would Jesus own a house or rent an apartment?* These are
all examples of the kind of decisions life demands that
we make. Ultimately, we must rely on our consciences to
make these types of decisions (1:12). There were many
decisions that Paul made in his relationship with the
Corinthians, some of which were great and others that
caused tension in his relationship with them. However,
Paul stood firm in his convictions that he had always dealt
with them in a holy and sincere way. Later in the letter he
appeals to their conscience, to their inner realization of
who he showed himself to be in his relationship with them
(5:11).

Paul refers to the conscience many times throughout
his writings. Often, as in this context (1:12), he uses it as
his standard to determine his guilt or innocence before
the Lord. (See Acts 23:1; 24:16.) Similarly, in 1 Corinthians
8, Paul is dealing with an issue that had become a problem in the early church—the eating of meat that had been

sacrificed to idols. To the pagan mind, eating this meat was a spiritual union between the person and the idol. Obviously, after becoming a Christian these pagan rituals should have been meaningless. However, after years of eating this sacrificed meat, the conscience of an idolater had been trained a certain way, making it very difficult for the young disciple to eat it with a clear conscience. Jesus declared that all food was clean (Matthew 15:17-20). Although there was nothing objectively wrong with eating this meat now that they were disciples, it still wounded their conscience:

> *Some people are still so accustomed to idols that when they eat such food they think of it as having been sacrificed to an idol, and since their conscience is weak, it is defiled (1 Corinthians 8:7).*

However, earlier in 1 Corinthians 4:4, Paul implies the inadequacy of the conscience in determining the will of God when he says, "My conscience is clear, but that does not make me innocent. It is the Lord who judges me." It almost sounds like Paul is contradicting himself. In one case Paul let his conscience be his guide, and in the other case, even though he felt innocent, he states that it is the Lord who judges. How can we be sure? When can we trust our feelings, and when should we not trust them?

I believe the answer lies in the reason God gave us our consciences. In Romans 2:14-15, as he does here in 1:12, Paul mentions the conscience bearing witness, either accusing us or defending us. A guilty conscience puts a heavy strain on our emotions. If our hearts are pure, our conscience forces us to search for the answers by studying the biblical foundation on which decisions are made, by seeking the counsel and advice of others, and by devoting ourselves to prayer. If we refuse to listen to our conscience and allow it to be "seared as with a hot iron" (1 Timothy

4:2), then we lose all hope of ever finding the will of God. A guilty conscience often tells us we are guilty. But sometimes when we feel guilty, in reality we are not, as in the case of the Corinthians eating meat that was sacrificed to idols. In every case, however, when we feel guilty, we must stop whatever we are doing and resolve the issue quickly. Failure to do this defiles the conscience, which jeopardizes its usefulness for future decisions. Thus, causing another disciple to defile his conscience is a serious matter to God: "When you sin against your brothers in this way and wound their weak conscience, you sin against Christ" (1 Corinthians 8:12).

Not Hard to Understand

> *13For we do not write you anything you cannot read or understand. And I hope that, 14as you have understood us in part, you will come to understand fully that you can boast of us just as we will boast of you in the day of the Lord Jesus.*

In Paul's first letter to the Corinthians he said, "When I came to you, brothers, I did not come with eloquence or superior wisdom as I proclaimed to you the testimony about God" (1 Corinthians 2:1). Paul was a highly educated man, well versed in Hebrew, Greek and Aramaic, and very knowledgeable about the Old Testament and the philosophies of his day. Yet Paul never used his knowledge to degrade or confuse others. Knowledge of God, knowledge of the word of God, knowledge of how to carry out his responsibilities in the kingdom and the like were some of his most prized possessions—and they must be ours as well.

On the other hand, Paul gives us important spiritual insight when he tells the Corinthians, "Knowledge puffs up, but love builds up" (1 Corinthians 8:1b). Knowledge alone is dangerous. Knowledge along with love is unbelievably powerful!

So much of both ancient—and modern—religion can be defined as arguing and dividing—doing what Paul refers to as "quarreling about words" (2 Timothy 2:14). This is an example of knowledge arguing against knowledge. Without love, knowledge is always destructive. Paul goes on to say that "it is of no value, and only ruins those who listen" (2 Timothy 2:14). However, in light of these scriptures we may be tempted to overreact and neither seek the deeper things of the Word nor appreciate the important detailed work of others whom God has used to provide us, for example, with translations of the Bible or insights from history that aid us in the study of the Word.

Describing the writings of Paul, Peter once wrote:

> *He writes the same way in all his letters, speaking in them of these matters. His letters contain some things that are hard to understand which ignorant and unstable people distort, as they do the other Scriptures, to their own destruction (2 Peter 3:16).*

Paul was a deep man, as is evident in his letter to the Romans, and sometimes dealing with deeper theological issues is the need of the hour. Yet in every case Paul wrote and used the knowledge that God had given him for building and strengthening the church and not for his own glory or for destructive purposes. An important passage in this regard is 1 Timothy 6:3-5:

> *If anyone teaches false doctrines and does not agree to the sound instruction of our Lord Jesus Christ and to godly teaching, he is conceited and understands nothing. He has an unhealthy interest in controversies and quarrels about words that result in envy, strife, malicious talk, evil suspicions and constant friction between men of corrupt mind, who have been robbed of the truth and who think that godliness is a means to financial gain.*

There are many warnings in the Bible against false teaching. True disciples of Christ must know the difference between true and false teachers. Ignorance profits no one and leaves us gullible and vulnerable to being deceived and being led away from the truth of God's word. An important key is found in 1 Corinthians 13:6, when Paul writes that love "rejoices with the truth." True disciples must seek the truth out of their love for God and for one another, no matter how deep that search takes them. (Certainly, we must be careful not to allow our search for truth to be used as a weapon against one another. Rather, we must learn to search together so that we can in unity draw close to God.)

Paul wrote to the Corinthians this time so that they might better understand him and the mission God had given him. It was Paul's hope that that would bring unity and a mutual boasting on the day of the Lord. True unity results in a deep blending of aspirations, dreams, victories and failures, along with all the corresponding emotions. Concerning this unified body of Christ, or the church, Paul wrote, "If one part suffers, every part suffers with it; if one part is honored, every part rejoices with it (1 Corinthians 12:26). Paul's relationship with the Corinthians was far from this ideal. Suspicion, distrust, criticism and jealousy were destroying any potential for genuine understanding and identification with the victories and disappointments in each other's lives.

Most often when there are conflicts in our relationships as Christians, or when we have been hurt by our brothers and sisters, we become defensive and begin to blame-shift. Not only that, but we stop listening and seeking to understand the other person's perspective and feelings. Paul's hope here is that the Corinthians would come to a full understanding of all of the spiritual dynamics that were determining the course and direction of his life. The Corinthians' only partial understanding of him was causing them to be critical, disrespectful and ungrateful. A full understanding of Paul, more specifically, being able to see Paul's love for them and how proud he was of them, would enable them to in turn *boast* about him and to be proud to be his children in the faith.

Worldly Planning?

> *15Because I was confident of this, I planned to visit you first so that you might benefit twice. 16I planned to visit you on my way to Macedonia and to come back to you from Macedonia, and then to have you send me on my way to Judea. 17When I planned this, did I do it lightly? Or do I make my plans in a worldly manner so that in the same breath I say, "Yes, yes" and "No, no"?*

1 Corinthians 16:1-9 mentions that Paul had planned to visit the Corinthians after his visit to Macedonia and on his way to Jerusalem. Because of God's overall plan, which Paul mentions later on in 2 Corinthians 1:8-11, Paul was detained in Macedonia. This change in travel plans was obviously a sharp point of contention in the hearts of the Corinthians. Paul is trying to show that it was his full intention to visit the Corinthians twice, because they were truly on Paul's heart. This was not simply an issue of the travel itinerary of a missionary revisiting his churches. It was an issue of the heart, which the Corinthians had failed to see. The amazing thing about criticism is its ability to conceal the truth. The Corinthian church saw fickleness and a lack of character and love in Paul rather than the agonizing and disappointing decision to change plans because of God's greater plan. How could a change in plans so quickly remove such a depth of love? Nothing had changed in Paul's heart—the only change was in his itinerary, which he had ultimately no control over.

Sometimes when we read the Bible, we lose sight of the fact that behind these letters was a fast-paced ministry with lots of problems and changes, much like the ministries most of us are involved in. But we need to realize that travel in the first century was much more difficult, exhausting and time-consuming than it is for us. Today we could travel around the world several times in the time it took for Paul to go from Macedonia to Corinth. The decision by Paul to change travel plans was in no way done in a casual or relaxed manner.

Just like what happened between Paul and the Corinthians, in our relationships in the church we end up hurting each other's feelings, as much as we try not to. Hurt feelings are the seedbed of critical thinking. It is nearly impossible to be objective when we are hurt. We begin to believe and draw conclusions about one another that are far removed from reality. Deep inside we may know the truth about the person who hurt us, but our hurt feelings suppress any possibility of that truth coming to our rescue. Oftentimes families become dysfunctional, marriages end in divorce, and children and parents end up hating each other for this very reason. Did the Corinthians actually *believe* that Paul made his plans like a man of the world? The man who had converted them and become their father in the faith? The man who literally had put his life in jeopardy in order to bring the Gospel to them? What happened to all of this truth in the hearts of the Corinthians?

Paul refers to the perceived "worldly manner" (1:17) with which the Corinthians had accused him of making his plans. The Greek word here is *sarx,* which is more often translated "flesh" in the New Testament. Paul is being accused of making his plans in a self-centered, ungodly way that is more indicative of the sinful nature than a spiritual way of thinking.

God Is Faithful

> *[18]But as surely as God is faithful, our message to you is not "Yes" and "No." [19]For the Son of God, Jesus Christ, who was preached among you by me and Silas and Timothy, was not "Yes" and "No," but in him it has always been "Yes." [20]For no matter how many promises God has made, they are "Yes" in Christ. And so through him the "Amen" is spoken by us to the glory of God. [21]Now it is God who makes both us and you stand firm in Christ. He anointed us, [22]set his seal of ownership on us, and put his Spirit in our hearts as a deposit, guaranteeing what is to come.*

Paul now turns to the spiritual truths that were a part of his decision-making process in his travel itinerary. For starters, the message that we have from Christ is not a mixed bag of spiritual goodies, controlled by temporal and transitory concerns and left to the winds of mere chance. In Paul's mind there are simply no negative aspects to the message of Jesus. For example, a change of plans for nondisciples can be a devastating and disappointing experience, but in Christ it is a door opening to something far greater.

Of all God's promises the ability to "stand firm in Christ" (1:21) must be regarded as God's greatest promise. We also have the promises (1:20) of eternal life, victory over sin, resurrection, the ability to build spiritual families and relationships, having an impact on the world, and more! All these promises are protected by God's unlimited power, and any change in our temporal plans simply means the better implementation and application of *God's* plans.

God is incapable of taking any steps backward and incapable of being defeated on any front. He always moves forward victoriously with a sensitive and aggressive plan which no mere change in our plans could ever alter. Even when our own personal sin seems to foil the plan of God, because of his mercy, he is able to reconstruct and rebuild our lives. Our repentance gives God another opportunity to accomplish his plan.

Many reputable scholars have taken the view that Paul, in this section (1:18-22), is defending the apostolic ministry that God had given him and is consequently referring to the anointing, sealing and the presence of the Spirit as evidence of his apostolic ministry.[1] However, this view fits neither the context nor the exact wording of the verses. Paul wrote, "Now it is God who makes *both us and you* stand firm in Christ" (1:21, emphasis added). Obviously, he is referring to both himself *and* the Corinthians. He is not trying to ram his apostolic authority down the throats of the Corinthians but rather he is trying to build a much needed and lost unity between them. They, together with him, are involved in the same ministry. Whatever happens to him, happens to them. Whenever he suffers, they should suffer. Whenever he is comforted, they are also comforted. The situation had tragically become that, when Paul suffered and consequently had to change his plans, they had become unsympathetic, distrustful and critical.

Throughout this section (1:18-22) it is clear that Paul's conviction was that he had to keep the Corinthians focused on Christ and God instead of allowing them to be consumed with the human side of ministry. The plans of men change—but the plans of God are consistent and faithful. As part of his argument, Paul introduces the work of the Holy Spirit as representing three separate but related functions: 1) an anointing, 2) a seal and 3) a deposit or guarantee.

The powerful biblical concept of "anointing" has its roots in the anointing of the ancient priests of Israel. God told Moses, "After you put these clothes on your brother Aaron and his sons, anoint and ordain them. Consecrate them so they may serve me as priests" (Exodus 28:41). The word is also used in reference to the ancient Jewish tabernacle: "Take the *anointing* oil and *anoint* the tabernacle and everything in it; consecrate it and all its furnishings, and it will be holy" (Exodus 40:9, emphasis added). Along with the priests and tabernacle, throughout the history of Israel, judges, prophets and kings were anointed for service to God.

"Anointing" has two basic meanings in the Scriptures. The first has to do with something or someone being chosen. As is obvious from Exodus 40:9 above, anointing is closely connected to holiness, which basically means the choosing or setting aside of something or someone for a particular purpose. Second, whatever was anointed was then called to fulfill the function for which it had been chosen. For example, the priests were anointed to serve the tabernacle and later the temple. No one else was allowed to carry out those duties except the ones who had been anointed. To God anointing was very serious. Notice the tone of this passage in Exodus 30:

> "Anoint Aaron and his sons and consecrate them so they may serve me as priests. Say to the Israelites, 'This is to be my sacred anointing oil for the generations to come. Do not pour it on men's bodies and do not make any oil with the same formula. It is sacred, and you are to consider it sacred. Whoever makes perfume like it and whoever puts it on anyone other than a priest must be cut off from his people'" (Exodus 30:30-33).

The Old Testament sets the stage for many of the concepts we find in the New Testament, and we must keep the OT background in mind when we read Jesus' quote from Isaiah as he refers to himself and his ministry in Luke 4:18-19:

> "The Spirit of the Lord is on me,
>   because he has anointed me
>   to preach good news to the poor.

> *He has sent me to proclaim freedom*
> *for the prisoners*
> *and recovery of sight for the blind,*
> *to release the oppressed,*
> *to proclaim the year of the Lord's favor."*

Jesus had been chosen to fulfill a specific ministry just as the priests, prophets and kings of the Old Testament had.

Originally, the word "Christ" (*Christos*) meant "the anointed one" or "messiah." It was used in that sense to refer to the belief among the Jews that a messiah or an anointed one would come to deliver God's people from foreign rule and set them up as their own nation again (Matthew 2:4; 22:42). Later the term "Christ" began to be used to refer to the man, Jesus of Nazareth, as in the discourse between the crowd and Pontius Pilate (Matthew 27:22). This evolved to the point that the early church referred to him simply as "Jesus Christ" (Acts 2:38; 3:6).

However, having looked at this historical background, we must move on and be practical. Do you as a disciple consider yourself anointed? Does it excite you to imagine being chosen and given a task in the same way that the ancient kings, priests and prophets were anointed? Unfortunately, for most Christians it is not the same emotional experience at all. Far too many disciples have the emotions of being chosen to live an agonizing life of self-denial, disappointing fruitlessness and constant challenges to repent. This is a sad reality, particularly in comparison to the rich background out of which the concept of anointing emerges, as well as the fact that what we have in Christ is far greater than anything the ancients were capable of having.

Paul emphasizes this point further by referring to being "sealed" by God (1:22). The Greek word *sfragidzo* is used in reference to sealing something so that it would not be disturbed. In Daniel 6:17 King Darius, after placing

Daniel in the lions' den, sealed the stone that had been placed over the den with his signet ring. Another meaning of "sealed" is "to mark something as a means of identification." All kinds of animals were sealed in this respect in the ancient world, which implied not only ownership but also the protection that goes along with being owned. Similarly, in Christ we are identified as God's children and protected by his power. (See Ephesians 1:13 and Revelation 7:3.)

Paul also uses the word "deposit," to describe the activity of the Holy Spirit (1:22). The Greek word is *arrabon*, which is defined as "first installment, deposit, down payment, pledge, that pays a part of the purchase price in advance, and so secures a legal claim to the article in question or makes a contract valid."[2] In other words, the Holy Spirit is God's down payment or deposit given to us guaranteeing what is to come. Unlike so many people who do not pay their bills after making down payments, God is incapable of not fulfilling his Word.

With the intensity of this imagery the Corinthians had no reason to lose heart and become critical of Paul. Regardless of Paul's actions, the Corinthians had promises of God already in their midst—with more to come. They had become too focused on people and had lost sight of the magnificence of God. The challenges are the same for us today. We will never be in the perfect church, have the perfect discipleship partner or the perfect ministry leader. Our evangelist could always preach a little better, be a little more spiritual, more understanding or more people-focused. Yet, none of these weaknesses deplete the strength, power and faithfulness of God. Weakness and inconsistency are part of our existence in a fallen world, and the only effective way to live with these realities is to see the big picture of God's working throughout history and through our individual lives in that history.

2

The Triumphal Procession

2 Corinthians 1:23-2:17

Even in the kingdom of God, misunderstandings will arise in relationships. The Corinthian disciples misinterpreted various actions of Paul—and even some of his directions. In this next section Paul addresses those misunderstandings and makes clear the love he has for the disciples. Most importantly, he expresses great confidence that in Christ, relationship issues can always be resolved and God's people can march on in triumphal procession.

We Work with You

> *1:23I call God as my witness that it was in order to spare you that I did not return to Corinth. 24Not that we lord it over your faith, but we work with you for your joy, because it is by faith you stand firm.*

Now Paul begins to reveal some of the other reasons why he had postponed his trip to Corinth (1:23-24). The letter of 1 Corinthians shows in greater detail how serious the problems were in the Corinthian congregation. Division, immorality, lack of spirituality, lack of doctrinal convictions and criticalness of Paul characterized the church. Things had even deteriorated to the point that the disciples were no longer eager to financially support Paul (1 Corinthians 9). Serious spiritual problems demand immediate and serious solutions. Paul writes:

> *Some of you have become arrogant, as if I were not coming to you. But I will come to you very soon, if the Lord is*

willing, and then I will find out not only how these arrogant
people are talking, but what power they have. For the king-
dom of God is not a matter of talk but of power. What do you
prefer? Shall I come to you with a whip, or in love and with
a gentle spirit? (1 Corinthians 4:18-21).

One thing is always clear in Paul's heart—his love for the people he ministered to and converted. Even though the Corinthians were not willing to support Paul in the ministry, he did not exercise his right as an apostle to demand their support. This is a key to great spiritual leadership. Having the right to do something does not always mean it is the right thing to do. Notice Paul's attitude:

But we did not use this right. On the contrary, we put up
with anything rather than hinder the gospel of Christ.... But
I have not used any of these rights. And I am not writing this
in the hope that you will do such things for me. I would rather
die than have anyone deprive me of this boast (1 Corinthians
9:12, 15).

As we have discussed earlier, the Corinthians had concluded from Paul's postponement of his trip to see them that he was either fickle and inconsistent or that he simply did not care about their needs. On the contrary, Paul calls God as his witness that one of his reasons for not coming was to spare the Corinthians the discipline that they deserved (1:23). There is a great spiritual lesson here. It is obvious from the Bible that repentance must be an expectation of all leaders, both in their own lives and in the lives of those they lead. However, repentance can never be forced.

In this case it seems like Paul was trying to foster the type of environment best suited for the Corinthians to come to their senses. Confrontation is not always the best motivation for repentance. Oftentimes, disciples need time to reflect on where their real convictions lie. The

Corinthians knew how Paul had treated them and how he had always striven to feed and nourish them. If that truth was powerless in contributing to a genuine change of heart, then what could Paul expect from his being there? Paul trusted in the truth and wanted to give the disciples time to think about what he had written before he came to them. Success in the church is always a team effort, and Paul had put a plan into action which he believed would bring the team success:

Paul's Deep Love

> ²:¹So I made up my mind that I would not make another painful visit to you. ²For if I grieve you, who is left to make me glad but you whom I have grieved? ³I wrote as I did so that when I came I should not be distressed by those who ought to make me rejoice. I had confidence in all of you, that you would all share my joy. ⁴For I wrote you out of great distress and anguish of heart and with many tears, not to grieve you but to let you know the depth of my love for you.

As Paul's letter to the Romans is known for its depth and theology, the book of 2 Corinthians is known for revealing the heart of Paul. Though history has elevated Paul to an almost angelic status, it must be remembered that he was only a *man* with the same insecurities, fears and weaknesses as we have. The tension between him and the Corinthians was distressing to him, and any thought of separation was extremely discouraging. Paul considered his relationship to his converts to be like a father-child relationship. He stated in 1 Corinthians 4:14-15:

> I am not writing this to shame you, but to warn you, as my dear children. Even though you have ten thousand guardians in Christ, you do not have many fathers, for in Christ Jesus I became your father through the gospel.

As a loving father grieves as he disciplines his children, so did Paul grieve when thinking about dealing with the Corinthians. What was once such a tremendous joy had become a source of grief and frustration. The ideal of what the relationship should have been like is seen in Paul's relationship with the Philippians: "Therefore, my brothers, you whom I love and long for, my joy and crown, that is how you should stand firm in the Lord, dear friends!" (Philippians 4:1). It was this hope deferred that brought "great distress and anguish of heart and...many tears" to Paul's life (2:4).

Outwitting Satan

> *[5] If anyone has caused grief, he has not so much grieved me as he has grieved all of you, to some extent—not to put it too severely. [6] The punishment inflicted on him by the majority is sufficient for him. [7] Now instead, you ought to forgive and comfort him, so that he will not be overwhelmed by excessive sorrow. [8] I urge you, therefore, to reaffirm your love for him. [9] The reason I wrote you was to see if you would stand the test and be obedient in everything. [10] If you forgive anyone, I also forgive him. And what I have forgiven—if there was anything to forgive—I have forgiven in the sight of Christ for your sake, [11] in order that Satan might not outwit us. For we are not unaware of his schemes.*

In chapter 5 of 1 Corinthians Paul had rebuked the Corinthians for not dealing with a brother who was sleeping with his father's wife. This problem was in reality merely a symptom of a much wider and deeper spiritual problem. The arrogance of the Corinthians had blinded them to the seriousness of the sin and the destructive influence it was having on the church. Paul's commandment was:

> *When you are assembled in the name of our Lord Jesus and I am with you in spirit, and the power of our Lord Jesus is present, hand this man over to Satan, so that the sinful nature may be destroyed and his spirit saved on the day of the Lord (1 Corinthians 5:4-5).*

This verse has often been misunderstood and misapplied throughout history. In many denominational churches today sin is tolerated, and this command is ignored. The other extreme was seen in the Catholic church of the Middle Ages where the Greek word, *sarx,* which literally means "flesh," was interpreted to be the flesh of the physical body rather than the "sinful nature." Consequently, Catholics suspected of disobedience were tortured, by either being burned at the stake or being skinned alive, in order to prepare them spiritually for death. This is hardly what Paul had in mind in this passage! Yet what is important is to find out more exactly what Paul meant in 1 Corinthians 5 in order to understand the admonishment he gives in our present passage, 2:5-11.

The denominational world avoids 1 Corinthians 5:5 because of their false concept of tolerance and acceptance. Unlike the religious world, *life-style* in true Christianity makes a difference as to whether or not someone remains pleasing to God. If a disciple refuses to continue living the life that Jesus calls every disciple to live, then that person is not pleasing to God. If repentance does not take place, he or she will be lost. The seriousness of this situation is the backdrop to the action that Paul is calling for in 1 Corinthians 5. Handing a person over to Satan (or withdrawing fellowship) has the purpose of allowing a person to feel the full consequences of falling back into the world. Being out of relationship with other Christians is part of the process of bringing someone back to their senses and to true repentance. Disfellowship should never be done out of revenge, but always out of love.

We cannot know for sure, but it seems likely that the person under consideration in 2:5-11 is the same person who had been disfellowshipped in 1 Corinthians 5. Another possibility is that the Corinthians overall had repented in this area and had begun to deal with various situations in the church, which called for the disfellowshipping of several individuals. Whatever the circumstances, it is clear by the time of the writing of 2 Corinthians, the pendulum had swung the other way and forgiveness and encouragement were now the need of the hour. It was time to forgive and encourage the repentant disciple. As Paul had admonished in 1 Corinthians 5:3, "Even though I am not physically present, I am with you in spirit. And I have already passed judgment on the one who did this, just as if I were present," so he says in 2 Corinthians 2:10, "If you forgive anyone, I also forgive him. And what I have forgiven—if there was anything to forgive—I have forgiven in the sight of Christ for your sake." Thus, Paul's presence as an apostle was not necessary to deal with this situation, and the sin was not committed against Paul, but against the Lord and the church in Corinth. The important point here is that emphasizing forgiveness is just as important as dealing with sin in a hard-line way. Every church of Christ must not only maintain a hard-line position against sin but must also reflect the same spirit of forgiveness and grace that we see in the life of Jesus. Satan will attack us on both of these fronts; therefore we must be aware of them, "in order that Satan might not outwit us."

Desperately Seeking News

12Now when I went to Troas to preach the gospel of Christ and found that the Lord had opened a door for me, 13I still had no peace of mind, because I did not find my brother Titus there. So I said good-by to them and went on to Macedonia.

This passage has often been interpreted as showing the importance of relationships in the life of Paul. It is said that even though he had an open door to preach the gospel in Troas, Paul's need for time with Titus was more important to him. Though this interpretation is attractive in a world where so few have meaningful and lasting relationships, it does not really fit the context of what Paul is trying to do. In 2 Corinthians 7:5-7 Paul writes:

> For when we came into Macedonia, this body of ours had no rest, but we were harassed at every turn—conflicts on the outside, fears within. But God, who comforts the downcast, comforted us by the coming of Titus, and not only by his coming but also by the comfort you had given him. He told us about your longing for me, your deep sorrow, your ardent concern for me, so that my joy was greater than ever.

It is obvious from this passage the real reason Paul left Troas was to find Titus. While the Corinthians were accusing Paul of not caring, Paul was at the same time searching intensely for Titus, longing for encouraging news about the Corinthians. This shows how far off the mark we can be when, out of a critical attitude or hurt feelings, we judge another's heart. Good, solid communication is critical during the inevitable times of conflict in our relationships. In his heart, Paul was so far from the picture the Corinthians had painted of him. The very news that the Corinthians longed for him resulted in him saying, that "my joy was greater than ever" (2 Corinthians 7:7).

Satan is the master of painting pictures that have no connection with reality. These pictures destroy relationships, families, marriages and even the church of Christ. It takes courage and humility to break through all of the deception, false conclusions and pride that keep us from really seeing one another's hearts. The challenge for the Corinthians was that even though they had been hurt and disappointed by Paul's change of plans, they needed to push harder than ever to get to the truth of Paul's heart.

Sweet-Smelling Messengers

> *[14]But thanks be to God, who always leads us in trium-
> phal procession in Christ and through us spreads everywhere
> the fragrance of the knowledge of him.*

Paul's meeting with Titus is not picked up again until 7:5 which means the material from 2:14 through 7:4 must be studied, to some extent, as a long parenthetical statement. Yet, it will become clear how packed this section is with both rich theology and great insight into the heart of the apostle Paul.

As is clear in 2:14, Paul had gained the incredible ability to rejoice in the most stressful and challenging situations. Suffering is the time when the flesh and spirit battle for supremacy. The unspiritual person, who is dependent only on the flesh, becomes bitter, doubtful and hard when suffering. The spiritual person, on the other hand, is God-dependent, faithful and peaceful. The circumstances are the same, yet the responses and results are totally different.

Our responses and reactions to both suffering and intense challenges show us clearly where we are rooted. Paul's spirituality (2:14) reaches new heights in that, though he had been under intense pressure—even to the point of death as mentioned in 1:9—he had achieved a deep faith in the spiritual realities beyond the physical senses. In the eyes of the world Paul was on the brink of insanity. But to God and to himself, Paul was marching in a triumphal procession. And this procession is of a different sort than most disciples expect to experience. Most of us view life as a series of ups and downs, victories and defeats. In contrast Paul writes that God *"always* leads us in triumphal procession in Christ" (2:14). In this procession there is no defeat—only victory. We may not always *feel* as victorious as Paul at certain times in his life (again see 1:9), but we should be thankful that God's victory is not dependent on our feelings!

Where, then, do the defeats of life come in? The answer is simple: They don't! Defeat is as much a state of mind as it is an objective reality. Defeat to the Christian is simply a tool to achieve a higher degree of victory—a place where humility and servanthood are forged. It is an exciting learning process in which we are transformed in a greater way into the image of Christ.

There is little doubt that when Paul wrote about the "triumphal procession" (2:14), he had in mind a Roman victory parade in celebration of the winning of a war. His reference to "the fragrance of the knowledge of him" (2:14) could also be a reference to the smell of the incense that was burned along the path of ancient victory parades. Whatever the case, the image of a parade was a favorite one of Paul. Here he uses it to represent the opposite idea to the one found in 1 Corinthians 4:9:

> *For it seems to me that God has put us apostles on display at the end of the procession, like men condemned to die in the arena. We have been made a spectacle to the whole universe, to angels as well as to men.*

In this context he is emphasizing anything but victory. Yet, the contrast here makes the point clear how we can look at our circumstances in two different ways. 1 Corinthians 4:9 is clearly how Paul often felt in his ministry, rejected by men and the world—even the churches he planted at times had suspicious and unsupportive feelings towards him. Yet, feelings are often the last indication of reality. The flesh can make us feel something totally opposite to the realities we have in the spiritual realm. Jesus himself said,

> *"Blessed are those who are persecuted because of righteousness,*
> *for theirs is the kingdom of heaven.*

*"Blessed are you when people insult you, persecute you
and falsely say all kinds of evil against you because of me.
Rejoice and be glad, because great is your reward in heaven,
for in the same way they persecuted the prophets who were
before you" (Matthew 5:10-12).*

God views our being persecuted for his cause vastly
different from how the world views it. The wrath of the
world in the case at hand is a test of how firmly rooted
we are in the kingdom of God and in the fellowship of the
men and women who have given their lives for God.

The Aroma of Christ

*[15]For we are to God the aroma of Christ among those who
are being saved and those who are perishing. [16a]To the one
we are the smell of death; to the other, the fragrance of life.*

All of us have heard the saying, "Beauty is in the eyes
of the beholder." Something similar can be said of fragrances. This is very evident when we visit or live in a
another country or culture. We often walk into a country
and react to what we consider to be horrible and almost
sickening smells, only to find out that these smells are
totally normal—and even beautiful—fragrances to the
people there. What is the difference? Simply the conditioning of our senses. What smells good or bad to us is a
matter of what we have been raised with and what we
have been taught environmentally. For example, the smell
of pork ribs being barbecued is, to most Americans, a
sweet and beautiful smell. Yet, taking that barbecue pit to
the middle of Jerusalem would produce a entirely different reaction! Paul, in 2:15-16, is appealing to the same
truth concerning the message of Christ. Obviously, the
message of Christ produces different reactions in people
depending on the faith and perspective of the hearer. Paul
said in 1 Corinthians 1:22-25,

> *Jews demand miraculous signs and Greeks look for wisdom,*
> *but we preach Christ crucified: a stumbling block to Jews*
> *and foolishness to Gentiles, but to those whom God has*
> *called, both Jews and Greeks, Christ the power of God and*
> *the wisdom of God. For the foolishness of God is wiser than*
> *man's wisdom, and the weakness of God is stronger than*
> *man's strength.*

For a Jew to become a Christian in the first century meant having to work through and overcome very strong and nearly overpowering historical tradition and conditioning (and it still does). Though thousands of Jews became Christians in the first century, the courage to overcome these obstacles was a rarity among the Jewish people. The smell of death surrounding the crucifixion of Jesus was so strong to the Jewish nostrils that the fragrance of life had little chance to compete. On the other hand, the message of Christ to the believing mind was a sweet fragrance, even in the presence of the most intense persecution and threats of death.

What is important to keep in mind here is how all of this is connected to Paul's defense of his ministry to the Corinthian church. Paul and his ministry were quickly becoming the smell of death in the nostrils of the Corinthians. Their criticalness and lack of support were now becoming a sign of their impending doom. Their failure to acknowledge Paul as having been sent from God was the same as failing to accept God and his message.

Nonprofit Prophet

> [16b]*And who is equal to such a task?* [17]*Unlike so many, we do*
> *not peddle the word of God for profit. On the contrary, in*
> *Christ we speak before God with sincerity, like men sent from*
> *God.*

For a long time, I interpreted the phrase "And who is equal to such a task?" (2:16b) to reflect the humility of

Paul, in the sense that Paul could not believe that he had been chosen for such a task, and he felt a great sense of inadequacy about the ministry to which God had called him. However, after understanding a little more about the context and the overall purposes of the letter, it makes more sense to take this phrase in a rhetorical way. In other words, Paul's answer to his own question, "And who is equal to such a task?" would be, "I am!" Paul writes that he is not a peddler who depends on others for his survival and that he is not in it for the money—which, by the way, was apparently not coming from the Corinthians anyway! (See 1 Corinthians 9.) He had been sent from God and therefore was equal to any task that the Lord assigned him. The question in the beginning of 2 Corinthians 3, "Are we beginning to commend ourselves again?" (2:17), shows the probability that his confidence was more than likely going to be interpreted by the Corinthians as bragging and self-commendatory.

Heart-level communication, openness, forgiveness and ever-present confidence in God's sovereignty. These are all keys to great relationships in the kingdom of God, and Paul wanted to impress each of these on the Corinthians. Those who embrace these principles may seem out of touch, naive and foolish. They may smell like death to some with hardened hearts. But to those who see life through the cross of Christ, such is a fragrance that adds joy and meaning to life.

3

Transformed into His Likeness

2 Corinthians 3

It is quite amazing how ordinary human interaction can become the opportunity for the Spirit of God to reveal powerful truths. Paul's efforts to resolve and strengthen his relationship with the Corinthians leads him to a discussion of the glorious new covenant that they share in Christ. In the providence of God, seemingly mundane matters here lead to seeing more clearly the powerful, transforming work of the Spirit.

A Letter Written on Our Hearts

> *3:1Are we beginning to commend ourselves again? Or do we need, like some people, letters of recommendation to you or from you? 2You yourselves are our letter, written on our hearts, known and read by everybody. 3You show that you are a letter from Christ, the result of our ministry, written not with ink but with the Spirit of the living God, not on tablets of stone but on tablets of human hearts.*

His reference to the "letters of recommendation" (3:1) shows the formality and stiffness that had evolved between Paul and the Corinthians. Superficial relationships always have a shallow formality about them, signifying the lack of trust between parties. Paul is essentially asking the Corinthians, "Is this where we are? Have we regressed into the formality of needing letters of recommendation in order to trust and respect one another?"

It is amazing how many worldly relationships are held together by contracts, court injunctions, prenuptial agreements, child-visitation agreements, etc. All of these show the miserable failure of the world at building the quality of relationships God intends for us to have. True and lasting relationships begin in the heart—emotionally and communicatively.

If Paul were to ever need a formal letter of recommendation concerning the Corinthians, it would need to be the Corinthians themselves. They should be the ones to testify of the credibility and reliability of his life and ministry! They would not have even been disciples were it not for Paul's ministry. What brought Paul and the Corinthians together was the power of God, the incredible message of the gospel and the overall working of God throughout human history. Once they became disciples, they shared some special time with Paul laboring in the harvest field together.

Paul is beginning to draw an important contrast by using such phrases as "written not with ink but with the Spirit of the living God, not on tablets of stone but on tablets of human hearts" (3:3). Later he says, "He has made us competent as ministers of a new covenant" (3:6). He also says, "...not of the letter but of the Spirit; for the letter kills, but the Spirit gives life" (3:6). The contrast in all these cases is between the old and new covenant, tablets of stone and tablets of human hearts, and the letter versus the spirit. But what is Paul doing with this contrast, and how does it fit into his overall purpose for writing the letter?

Paul's mention of the "tablets of stone" (3:3) is an obvious reference to God giving Moses the tablets on which the Ten Commandments were written at Mt. Sinai. Therefore, the contrast here is between what happened at Sinai and what happened at Golgotha. This contrast cannot be understood without reference to Jewish history. Since Paul was a former Pharisee, we cannot fully understand him without understanding his Jewish heritage and the battles he fought in light of these contrasts. He recounted part of his religious résumé in Philippians 3:5-6:

> *...circumcised on the eighth day, of the people of Israel, of the tribe of Benjamin, a Hebrew of Hebrews; in regard to the law, a Pharisee; as for zeal, persecuting the church; as for legalistic righteousness, faultless.*

Paul was highly educated and thoroughly knowledgeable of Judaism, and after his conversion ironically spent a great deal of his energy combatting the teachings he had once defended. His letters to the Romans and to the Galatians show what a serious problem the teachings of Judaism had become to the young Christian church. The main problem was the emphasis the Jewish converts placed on the works of their old Jewish law as being necessary for salvation as disciples. Particularly, circumcision was touted as a requirement of salvation. The overall problem did not concern just one issue but involved two dichotomous ways of thinking and, consequently, of living.

Two passages from the Old Testament provide us with an important insight into the contrast that Paul is making. In Jeremiah 31:31-34 the prophet said,

> *"The time is coming," declares the* LORD,
>   *"when I will make a new covenant*
> *with the house of Israel*
>   *and with the house of Judah.*
> *It will not be like the covenant*
>   *I made with their forefathers*
> *when I took them by the hand*
>   *to lead them out of Egypt,*
> *because they broke my covenant,*
>   *though I was a husband to them,"*
>   *declares the* LORD.
> *"This is the covenant I will make*
>   *with the house of Israel*
>   *after that time," declares the* LORD.

"I will put my law in their minds
*   and write it on their hearts.*
I will be their God,
*   and they will be my people.*
No longer will a man teach his neighbor,
*   or a man his brother, saying, 'Know the* Lord,*
because they will all know me,
*   from the least of them to the greatest,"*
*   declares the* Lord.
"For I will forgive their wickedness
*   and will remember their sins no more."*

The second passage is found in Ezekiel 36:26-27:

"'I will give you a new heart and put a new spirit in you; I
will remove from you your heart of stone and give you a
heart of flesh. And I will put my Spirit in you and move you
to follow my decrees and be careful to keep my laws. You
will live in the land I gave your forefathers; you will be my
people, and I will be your God.'"

It is obvious from these passages, as well as many others, that the Old Testament was prophetically pointing to a time when God was going to give his people a new covenant and a new heart. The Old Testament, particularly the covenant at Mount Sinai, was never intended to be God's perfect and final will. It was simply a preparatory measure to keep the Jewish people together and somewhat civilized until the coming of the Messiah and the new covenant. The old covenant was never able to completely deal with the heart and was certainly not able to secure the permanent forgiveness of sins, which is why it needed to be fulfilled and replaced. (Hebrews chapters 8 through 10 contain an excellent treatment of these ideas.)

The old covenant was of such a nature that men tended to use it legalistically. In particular, problems in business or family relationships were solved by appealing to the principle of the law. The concepts of forgiveness, going the extra mile and being wronged in order to preserve a relationship were not the primary considerations of the old covenant. Because of their criticalness, the Corinthians were judging just like a Pharisee would judge someone who had broken the law. But Paul's ministry was not a result of the law but was a result of the Spirit. The change in his travel plans meant to the Corinthians that he had broken the "law" and there was no room for grace or forgiveness in their system. Paul's reference to the Corinthians being "a letter from Christ" reflects the amazing patience and vision Paul had for his children.

The contrast Paul is making between "tablets of stone" and "a letter from Christ" shows in many ways the height from which the Corinthians were in danger of falling. It is always amazing to me how Paul, even in the midst of some serious and painful criticism, continues to encourage the Corinthians and remind them of what God had done for them. This is the same type of relationship dynamic Paul had experienced in Judaism. The Pharisees were incredibly critical and unforgiving, and it seems in this context that the behavior of the Corinthians reminded him of his past life. It was time for the Corinthians to move from "tablets of stone" to "tablets of human hearts."

Life from the Spirit

> *⁴Such confidence as this is ours through Christ before God. ⁵Not that we are competent in ourselves to claim anything for ourselves, but our competence comes from God. ⁶He has made us competent as ministers of a new covenant— not of the letter but of the Spirit; for the letter kills, but the Spirit gives life.*

In verses 4 through 6 Paul expresses his confidence in being a minister of the new covenant, but it was not his performance under the law that qualified him to have this ministry as a disciple of Jesus. When Paul writes, "not of the letter...for the letter kills," he is emphasizing, as he does in all of his teaching, that he is not qualified according to the law. It is through God's grace that he is qualified to serve as a minister. One of the chief purposes of the law was to show how sinful we are (Romans 3:20). Everyone breaks the law, so if it were the law that determined our qualification to serve God, then no one would be able to serve! Paul's only claim and boast was in how great, powerful and gracious God is.

More and More Glory

> [7]Now if the ministry that brought death, which was engraved in letters on stone, came with glory, so that the Israelites could not look steadily at the face of Moses because of its glory, fading though it was, [8]will not the ministry of the Spirit be even more glorious? [9]If the ministry that condemns men is glorious, how much more glorious is the ministry that brings righteousness! [10]For what was glorious has no glory now in comparison with the surpassing glory. [11]And if what was fading away came with glory, how much greater is the glory of that which lasts!

Oftentimes when we study the New Testament and compare its message with the Law that was given to Moses at Mt. Sinai, it is easy to lose our appreciation for this great historical event and for God's purpose for it. Paul describes the ministry of Moses in terms of a "ministry that brought death" (3:7), and yet, in the same breath Paul says that the giving of the law "came with glory" (3:7). It is important to remember that Paul was a Jew and had for most of his life studied and defended Judaism. What took place at Mt. Sinai was to the Jew a glorious part of his past. It was also a glorious part of God's preparation for the coming of his Son, though this idea may have escaped many then and today.

It is very characteristic of Paul to show the weaknesses of the law and to argue persuasively for the need for the law to be fulfilled in Christ. At the same time Paul makes sure that his readers understand the greatness of the history of God's people. Notice what he does in Romans 9:1-5:

> *I speak the truth in Christ—I am not lying, my conscience confirms it in the Holy Spirit—I have great sorrow and unceasing anguish in my heart. For I could wish that I myself were cursed and cut off from Christ for the sake of my brothers, those of my own race, the people of Israel. Theirs is the adoption as sons; theirs the divine glory, the covenants, the receiving of the law, the temple worship and the promises. Theirs are the patriarchs, and from them is traced the human ancestry of Christ, who is God over all, forever praised! Amen.*

Though Paul graciously tips his hat as he moves through the incredible God-driven history of the Jewish people, it must be underscored that he is not drawing a contrast here between the old and the new with the purpose of showing the merits of both sides of the contrast. His purpose is clear: to show unequivocally the surpassing greatness of what he had received in the Spirit as compared to the critical, legalistic way of living. Paul has given us some of the most important and in-depth theology found anywhere in the Bible, but each of his letters was written to resolve an important practical problem among the churches for which he was responsible. Paul is trying to point the Corinthians away from their legalism to what they could become by embracing the ministry of the Spirit.

The Unveiling

> *[12]Therefore, since we have such a hope, we are very bold. [13]We are not like Moses, who would put a veil over his face to keep the Israelites from gazing at it while the radiance was fading away. [14]But their minds were made dull, for to this day the same veil remains when the old covenant is read. It has not been removed, because only in Christ is it taken away. [15]Even to this day when Moses is read, a veil covers their hearts. [16]But whenever anyone turns to the Lord, the veil is taken away.*

The word "therefore" in this context (3:12) must be taken seriously because it signals an important transition between more in-depth theological material and practical personal response. Paul writes that because of what we have in Christ, there is now hope—implying that up to the time of Christ, no real hope existed. The basic need for hope in life drove the Jews to try to find it in the law they had been given. Yet, law and hope form an illegitimate marriage. They can never get along! Law ultimately produces one thing: guilt. Hope must be derived from a totally different source. That is why Paul said,

> *Before this faith came, we were held prisoners by the law, locked up until faith should be revealed. So the law was put in charge to lead us to Christ that we might be justified by faith. Now that faith has come, we are no longer under the supervision of the law (Galatians 3:23-25).*

Once true faith and hope are revealed, law becomes unnecessary and unwanted. It becomes despised and rejected because of its inability to produce the inner life that we were created to experience. Law is simply a reminder of where we are, of what we cannot achieve on our own, and of where we should not want to return. It is no longer a satisfactory standard. It produces only legalism, competitiveness, frustration and a constant sense of guilt. Those who try to live under it and find meaning must undergo the most rigorous self-deception in order to survive its condemning message. They will always view others with the same frustration as they experience.

On the other hand, the boldness which is the result of the hope Paul writes about (3:12) is the ability to embrace the challenges of God and his message. With it we can dream, try new types of ministry, make mistakes, confess our faults and weaknesses to one another, readjust our plans, and, as in Paul's case, even change travel plans and still have the confidence that God is working in our lives.

For Paul to write, "We are not like Moses" (3:13) cut against the ultimate Jewish dream. The Exodus—that is Moses leading the Israelites out of Egyptian bondage—was one of the greatest moments in Israel's history. The only other time when more miracles were worked was during the time of Christ himself. Moses was one of the only people in human history to speak to God face to face. He was known as God's friend, actually seeing the back of God! He was the hero of every Jewish boy and girl. But now Paul wants to emphasize that someone far greater has taken center stage.

The focus of these verses (3:12-16) is the veil that Moses covered his face with, as recorded in Exodus 34:33-35. After he had received the Ten Commandments on the stone tablets, he returned to the Israelites. His face was so radiant that Aaron and rest of the Israelites could not look at it, so he covered it with a veil. Here in 2 Corinthians, Paul is obviously using that veil to represent an obstacle standing between whoever attempts to follow the old covenant and the glory of God. This veil is still like a covering, but not on the physical face. It now represents a covering of the mind and the heart, which are dulled and made hard when studying the old covenant.

Divine Transformation

> *[17]Now the Lord is the Spirit, and where the Spirit of the Lord is, there is freedom. [18]And we, who with unveiled faces all reflect the Lord's glory, are being transformed into his likeness with ever-increasing glory, which comes from the Lord, who is the Spirit.*

Paul is emphasizing that we have now entered into the age of the Spirit in contrast to the age of the law. Though the Holy Spirit was definitely at work during the time of the Old Testament, there is a sharp transition in his ministry after the coming of Jesus. This is alluded to in John 7:38-39:

> "Whoever believes in me, as the Scripture has said, streams of living water will flow from within him." By this he meant the Spirit, whom those who believed in him were later to receive. Up to that time the Spirit had not been given, since Jesus had not yet been glorified.

The Spirit had been working, but he had not yet been given. The giving of the Spirit came on the day of Pentecost when Peter said,

> "Repent and be baptized, every one of you, in the name of Jesus Christ for the forgiveness of your sins. And you will receive the gift of the Holy Spirit. The promise is for you and your children and for all who are far off—for all whom the Lord our God will call" (Acts 2:38-39).

The sharp difference between the Old Testament and the New Testament is that now we, as disciples, have the Spirit living *within* us. Prior to Christ, the Holy Spirit worked with only specific individuals, like Moses, but now we all reflect the Lord's glory.

Paul writes about "being transformed into his [the Lord's] likeness with ever-increasing glory" (3:18). In other words, the transformation of our lives is the practical demonstration of our encounter with the Lord's glory. The glory of God was revealed to the Jews as something mysterious and unattainable. In the letter to the Hebrews, the author conveyed in vivid terms what the presence of the Lord meant to the average Jew:

> You have not come to a mountain that can be touched and that is burning with fire; to darkness, gloom and storm; to a trumpet blast or to such a voice speaking words that those who heard it begged that no further word be spoken to

them, because they could not bear what was commanded:
"If even an animal touches the mountain, it must be stoned."
The sight was so terrifying that Moses said, "I am trembling
with fear" (Hebrews 12:18-21).

The glory and presence of God were terrifying to the Jewish people. They were a constant reminder of what they themselves were not able to become or attain and how far they were from God. Jesus, on the other hand, brought the glory of God near by his presence: "The Word became flesh and made his dwelling among us. We have seen his glory, the glory of the One and Only, who came from the Father, full of grace and truth" (John 1:14).

Under the new covenant, the glory of God is no longer just something that amazes or perplexes us. When we are eager and teachable, it shines into our lives in ever-increasing ways and changes us so that we become more and more like Christ.

4

Treasure in Jars of Clay

2 Corinthians 4:1-5:5

In his relationship with the Corinthians Paul had experienced no shortage of ups and downs. In his interactions with them, as with other churches, he knew times of hurt, confusion and discouragement. However, twice in 2 Corinthians 4 he makes it clear why he refuses to lose heart. Though he is a human vessel vulnerable to the vicissitudes of life and the fickleness of people, he had God who was working and preparing something beyond words for those who remained faithful.

We Have This Ministry

> *4:1Therefore, since through God's mercy we have this ministry, we do not lose heart.*

The word "ministry" means different things to different people. Growing churches often talk in terms of "moving the ministry," which means multiplying the ministry or adding to the number of disciples. When we say that we need to "minister to the needs of those around us," we usually mean serving others and helping them to deal with the pressures of life. However, in this context Paul uses the word to mean the ministry of the Spirit (3:8) that results in the inner transforming of our lives to conform to the standard given us in Jesus Christ. Because of this definition, Paul is able to say, "we do not lose heart." It is truly ironic how many disciples have it the opposite way. It is *because* of their ministry (defined as success in adding disciples) that so many disciples lose heart. Their ministry is not the source of their gaining heart and conviction, but it is the source of their discouragement and disappointment.

In order to avoid this burnout, it is important to define things *biblically* and not humanistically. The failure to obtain a particular goal for a certain period of time is not always an indication that disciples are not being transformed according to the image of Jesus Christ. In fact, times like these are often a great opportunity to grow in our perseverance, faith, trustworthiness and patience. Too much of a preoccupation with the achievement of goals reflects an unspiritual and humanistic results-oriented mentality. For example, it is possible to bring someone to the Lord and still not grow spiritually—or even take some serious spiritual steps backward by impure motives or a self-centered, self-glorifying heart.

> *[2]Rather, we have renounced secret and shameful ways; we do not use deception, nor do we distort the word of God. On the contrary, by setting forth the truth plainly we commend ourselves to every man's conscience in the sight of God.*

Because of Paul's focus on the quality of the Corinthians' life, that is, their conforming to the image of God's son, deception and distortion were out of the question. Transformation cannot be attained by deceitful, manipulative tactics. The very goal of transformation prohibits the use of these methods. Just as a surgeon's goal of keeping his patient infection-free assumes the use of disinfected surgical tools, so our goal of bringing people closer to the image of Jesus Christ assumes a conviction of pure and undefiled motives and methodology. Too many disciples focus on their methodology of ministry rather than a quality of teaching and righteous living. If we do not trust the truth of God's word to change hearts, then we trust in ourselves. Jesus said that it is the truth that sets people free (John 8:31-32)—not us and not our methodology. Good ministry methodology is the creative application of the truth. This is where Paul found his heart and confidence. This conviction is what kept Paul from the discouragement that many of us experience as we labor in the kingdom. Knowing that we are committed to the truth of God's word needs to provide us with an amazing amount of spiritual confidence and endurance. On the other hand, going to the Bible and twisting the meaning of a verse in order to hold on to a tradition must be unheard of in the true church of Christ!

They Cannot See

> [3]And even if our gospel is veiled, it is veiled to those who are perishing. [4]The god of this age has blinded the minds of unbelievers, so that they cannot see the light of the gospel of the glory of Christ, who is the image of God.

It is so easy to lose faith and become discouraged when people do not respond positively to the message of the gospel or our invitation to study the Bible. Sometimes it feels as if we are the ones perishing and not the unbelievers! Is that the response that God wants us to have? When someone rejects the gospel, it is evidence of the fact that they are the ones perishing, not us. It is evidence of the power of Satan to blind the minds of people, but it is not evidence of his power over us. It is only when we allow ourselves to be controlled by "results" or legalistic thinking that we end up feeling more miserable than the people we are trying to reach. When people reject the message of the gospel, the fact that they are perishing must produce more sympathy and love in our hearts for *them* and not sadness for ourselves (unless, of course, our motives are impure and self-centered)!

Satan's influence and control over the thinking of our world is immense and much more powerful than we could ever imagine. The very fact that, as disciples, we have been set free from his control and the imprisonment of our sinful natures through the death, burial and resurrection of Christ should bring us to an exhilarated level of joy and gratitude. To be able to see God in this dark, sinful world by "the light of the gospel of the glory of Christ" (4:4) is one of the greatest gifts we can possess. This gratitude and understanding are what fueled the fire beneath the ministry of the apostle Paul and kept his heart encouraged during some of the most intense trials that God has allowed any man to go through.

Not Ourselves, but Jesus

5For we do not preach ourselves, but Jesus Christ as Lord, and ourselves as your servants for Jesus' sake.

As one peels the layers off an onion, so in this series of passages Paul continues to peel away at the truths surrounding the credibility of his ministry. It is very easy in the twentieth century to open the Bible and show others that our message is rooted in the Bible. Then we can feel confident that if they have a problem with the message, their problem is with the Bible and not with us. That was not the exact case in Paul's situation—there was no New Testament to appeal to at that time. The New Testament had not yet been totally written and put together as we have it today, because God was still in the process of revealing his complete will after sending his Son. But Jesus promised that it would be completed: "'But when he, the Spirit of truth, comes, he will guide you into *all* truth'" (John 16:13, emphasis added).

In the first century, there was much more of a connection between who Paul was and the content of his message. So, if the Corinthians were having a problem with Paul personally, they would also be having a problem with his message. This is a large part of the reason

Paul spends so much time in both 1 and 2 Corinthians defending his apostleship—it was his apostleship that gave his message its authority.

In this verse (4:5) Paul is making the point that in the preaching of his message, he is not promoting himself and making himself out to be the standard. By holding up Jesus Christ as Lord, he was in reality serving the Corinthians and not enforcing his own authority. By the preaching of the gospel, Paul was not only serving the Lord, but was serving the Corinthians as well.

In our flesh, we are all rebellious and hate authority. Therefore, when we are doing poorly spiritually, the authority that God represents for our good ends up causing us to feel trapped, abused, victimized and constrained. We lose our perspective and no longer see God as serving us but as controlling our lives with a hidden agenda. This is exactly why the tension between Paul and the Corinthians was so tragic. Paul was the Corinthians' spiritual father, and yet because they had listened to the false teachers in Corinth and had become critical and ungrateful, they were now separated from Paul the same way that a dysfunctional family becomes distant and unloving. Though there is some indication that the process of repentance had begun (7:11-16), the influence of the false teachers on the Corinthians was not fully eradicated (see chapters 10-11). There was no one in the world that loved the Corinthians more than Paul, and yet, all of that love was seemingly powerless in helping the Corinthians see the light.

> [6]*For God, who said, "Let light shine out of darkness," made his light shine in our hearts to give us the light of the knowledge of the glory of God in the face of Christ.*

There is a good probability that Paul is here referring to the creation account in Genesis 1:3 when God said, "Let there be light," even though the wording is different.

Regardless, Paul is describing God as the power who brings the light of the gospel to a dark and dying world. Throughout the Bible there is the theme of the light in contrast to the darkness (see John 1:4; 3:19; Ephesians 5:8-14; 1 John 1:5). Here we have the light connected with the knowledge of the glory of God in contrast to the physical light of Genesis 1. The light, knowledge and glory of God are now seen in the face of Christ:

> *And he made known to us the mystery of his will according to his good pleasure, which he purposed in Christ, to be put into effect when the times will have reached their fulfillment—to bring all things in heaven and on earth together under one head, even Christ (Ephesians 1:9-10).*

Only in Christ does God make everything that was once abstract and unknown understandable, sensible and practical.

Treasure in Jars of Clay

> *[7]But we have this treasure in jars of clay to show that this all-surpassing power is from God and not from us. [8]We are hard pressed on every side, but not crushed; perplexed, but not in despair; [9]persecuted, but not abandoned; struck down, but not destroyed. [10]We always carry around in our body the death of Jesus, so that the life of Jesus may also be revealed in our body. [11]For we who are alive are always being given over to death for Jesus' sake, so that his life may be revealed in our mortal body. [12]So then, death is at work in us, but life is at work in you.*

Paul now refers to the knowledge of God which we have in Christ as "treasure" (4:7). However, this treasure is not found where most earthly valuables are kept. This treasure is found in "jars of clay" (4:7), which makes the contrast between the contents and the container the center of Paul's point.

This irony opens an important window into the character of God and how God has worked throughout human history. We have all heard the saying that God moves in mysterious ways. Though consistent, faithful, trustworthy and logical, God is never completely predictable. For example, righteousness and spirituality are seldom found among the attractive and recognized people and places of the world. Joseph was a slave, Moses a criminal in exile, David a shepherd boy, and Jesus a carpenter's son— and then there was also John the Baptist, living in the desert and eating locusts and wild honey!

Back when Moses led the Israelites out of Egyptian bondage, they were slaves oppressed by the most powerful nation in the world. Yet, because it is God's nature to create, transform and deliver, the weak become strong, and what is dead becomes alive. Consequently, what happens to a jar of clay in God's hands is totally different from anything possible in the world. Notice how Paul phrases this truth in 1 Corinthians 1:26-31,

> *Brothers, think of what you were when you were called.*
> *Not many of you were wise by human standards; not many*
> *were influential; not many were of noble birth. But God chose*
> *the foolish things of the world to shame the wise; God chose*
> *the weak things of the world to shame the strong. He chose*
> *the lowly things of this world and the despised things—and*
> *the things that are not—to nullify the things that are, so that*
> *no one may boast before him. It is because of him that you are*
> *in Christ Jesus, who has become for us wisdom from God—*
> *that is, our righteousness, holiness and redemption. There-*
> *fore, as it is written: "Let him who boasts boast in the Lord."*

Now let's put all of this in the context of 2 Corinthians. In chapter 1 Paul writes about how God allowed him to be brought almost to the point of death in order that he might learn a deeper level of God-reliance (1:8-9). Then in chapter 4, Paul writes about the "jars of clay"—an obvious reference to our flesh or humanity, which the Bible describes as weak, frail and sinful—the perfect place for God to demonstrate his power.

When the Corinthian church focused on Paul's flesh or humanness and consequently his weakness, rather than on God's power working through him, they were missing the point. They saw a man "hard pressed" rather than a man "not crushed." They saw a man "perplexed" rather than a man "not in despair" (4:8). The Corinthians should have been amazed at Paul's unbelievable God-given ability to victoriously endure the intense challenges that he was facing. Their focus on his flesh was destroying the beautiful bond that had once characterized their relationship with Paul. Our humanity should never be a dominant factor in our spiritual relationships—especially in our evaluation of each other.

Paul gives us a different slant on the practical application of the cross in our lives when he writes, "We always carry around in our body the death of Jesus, so that the life of Jesus may also be revealed in our body" (4:10). The primary purpose for the cross of Jesus is to provide for the forgiveness of our sins. But the resulting life of discipleship inspired by the cross demonstrates the gospel to the world. Paul's experience shows that the power is not only associated with a coming resurrection only to be experienced when Jesus returns, but also a practical daily ability to answer the call of discipleship in this life. The ultimate challenge for the disciple of Jesus is the experience of "always being given over to death for Jesus' sake" (4:11). Without the proper understanding of the purpose for this death—death to self—we will either despondently surrender to it or bitterly gnash our teeth when that death knocks on our door. However, with a right heart toward discipleship, as in the case of Paul, death to the world brings life to a dying world!

Paul puts two words together that normally do not go together, the Greek words for "flesh" (translated as "body" in the NIV) and "life." From a biblical perspective, normally flesh—or the sinful nature—destroys the spiritual life or the life destroys the flesh. Here it is the flesh that provides the possibility for the germination of the life of God. Life in this sense cannot be defined without the existence of the flesh. The flesh and its experience is where the miracle occurs. It is the primary place where God leaves the natural order of things and breaks into human history. As one disciple gives his life to the cause of God and dies to himself, others find the life they need to repeat the process. Paul's point to the Corinthians is that the death that they observed working in his life, and for which they had become critical of him, was in reality and ironically responsible for the life that they were enjoying (4:12).

Conviction That Must Be Expressed

> [13]*It is written: "I believed; therefore I have spoken." With that same spirit of faith we also believe and therefore speak,* [14]*because we know that the one who raised the Lord Jesus from the dead will also raise us with Jesus and present us with you in his presence.* [15]*All this is for your benefit, so that the grace that is reaching more and more people may cause thanksgiving to overflow to the glory of God.*

Paul's quotation of Psalm 116:10 (4:13) is a excellent illustration of how important the context of a passage is to the intent of a biblical author. Many times a New Testament writer using an Old Testament scripture not only had in mind the actual ideas found in the scripture quoted, but was also referring to the ideas found in the context of that particular passage. Therefore, in this case it is very important to read Psalm 116 entirely in order to better understand what Paul has in mind.

The theme of Psalm 116 is the praise of God for his deliverance during the most trying of times, as we can see from the verses quoted here:

> *The cords of death entangled me,*
> *the anguish of the grave came upon me;*
> *I was overcome by trouble and sorrow.*
> *Then I called on the name of the LORD:*
> *"O LORD, save me!"*
>
> *The LORD is gracious and righteous;*
> *our God is full of compassion.*
> *The Lord protects the simplehearted;*
> *when I was in great need, he saved me (Psalm 116:3-6).*

This psalm describes perfectly what Paul had experienced in Asia (1:8) and the incredible gratitude he had for God's deliverance. Psalm 116 is a song full of confidence that the Lord is good—a confidence which has come from the experience of deliverance.

There is one small difference between Paul and the psalmist, however. The psalmist is confident *after* the fact of deliverance. He writes, "when I was in great need, he saved me," and also, "For you, O Lord, have delivered my soul from death" (vv. 6, 8). Paul, on the other hand, praises God out of the confidence of what God is *going* to do. In 4:14, Paul writes, "because we know that the one who raised the Lord Jesus from the dead will also raise us with Jesus and present us with you in his presence." Paul is referring to what God is going to do on the last day, or the judgment day. He had already mentioned this to the Corinthians in 1 Corinthians 15 in his great chapter on the resurrection of Christ and to the church in Thessalonica, as well, in 1 Thessalonians 4:13-18.

Paul's emphasis in our current passage (4:13-15) is probably found in the words "and present us with you" (4:14). He is trying to again point the Corinthian church to the spiritual realities beyond the immediate circumstances. There is going to be a time when we are going to be raised with Christ and presented with him in the presence of God. This is the ultimate reality which can never be affected by temporal circumstances unless we, by our failure to repent, allow it to happen. These spiritual truths have power over the flesh. We cannot let the flesh take them from us! The picture of being together in God's presence forever ought to provide the motivation and reason to resolve our conflicts and repent of our criticalness of each other in the church.

What Paul had experienced and was presently enduring when he wrote 2 Corinthians was all for the purpose of giving the Corinthians the chance of participating in the most incredible, incomprehensible and unimaginable moment in all of history and in all of eternity. He stresses that "all this is for your benefit." God's plan is to demonstrate how his power is able to reach more and more people, causing more and more gratefulness in the world, despite what most would call insurmountable odds and obstacles.

No Loss of Heart

> [16]*Therefore we do not lose heart. Though outwardly we are wasting away, yet inwardly we are being renewed day by day.* [17]*For our light and momentary troubles are achieving for us an eternal glory that far outweighs them all.*

Having heart or losing heart (4:16) is an issue of the *contents* of our hearts, of what we treasure as valuable. Jesus said, "For where your treasure is, there your heart will be also" (Matthew 6:21). When we treasure what is occurring in the spiritual realm more than what is happening in the physical world around us, we can courageously face difficult circumstances. Changing our surroundings in an attempt to alleviate the pressures placed on our hearts can never effectively keep us from losing heart—we merely postpone the inevitable test of what's inside.

Jesus promises that the storms of life will hit each of us (Luke 6:46-49). The reality of "wasting away" (4:16) cannot be overcome by manipulating our circumstances. No matter what level of comfort we reach, we are all still "wasting away" and heading toward death. Some of us might fly economy class and some of us might have the privilege of flying first class, but we are all headed to the same airport. Protecting the heart is an inward battle. Losing heart is a failure to grasp the spiritual and eternal truths that God has revealed to us. The footsteps of Jesus were never meant to be easy and cannot be manipulated or customized to comfort the pain. The only real comfort lies in where those footsteps are leading: heaven!

Our understanding of the eternal and lasting truths to which Jesus leads us will determine whether we fall or keep walking. The outward wasting away of our humanity was meant to open for us the curtain to the reality of the home that Jesus has gone to prepare (John 14:1-4). How can we truly compare eternal glory with the suffering of this life? Even Jesus, as he faced the inevitability of the cross and its intense suffering, wrestled before God in an attempt to change his situation through prayer. Humanity definitely has a way of bringing us to our knees. Yet, Jesus found the power to hold on to the eternal truths waiting for him on the other side of the cross. We can see the suffering of this life as "light and momentary" not by removing the crosses of our existence, but by embracing them. Then God has the opportunity to reveal himself as the God of all comfort and as a God who ultimately raises the dead.

> [18]*So we fix our eyes not on what is seen, but on what is unseen. For what is seen is temporary, but what is unseen is eternal.*

"Fixing our eyes" (4:18) requires a decision. As spiritual people, we must determine and decide what we see, and not let it be determined for us. Seeing the unseen is a contradiction in terms. Paul is using wordplay to make the point that the power of the eternal is available only to the spiritually minded. Seeing the unseen is not a physical, but a spiritual, dynamic.

The irony of our existence is that the immediate world around us often determines so much of what we are, yet is referred to by Paul as temporary. Why do we allow the temporary to have such an impact in our lives? If life and its circumstances are temporary then that means they are going to pass. The power of the temporary in our lives is amazing. If we are to not lose heart, the eternal must become as real and near to us as the physical existence surrounding us. The tragedy is that most people allow the temporary to become their eternal. Their sense of success, contentment and overall well-being is found in their physical circumstances. But at the same time they have this gnawing unavoidable realization that what they have been using as their standard is quickly and irreversibly passing away. All of the material blessings and comforts of this life, even for the most hardened sinner, can never completely douse the heat of that burning realization.

> 5:1*Now we know that if the earthly tent we live in is destroyed, we have a building from God, an eternal house in heaven, not built by human hands.*

The phrase "now we know" is key here (5:1). Many Christians find themselves in a dilemma between their perceived problem between faith and knowledge. In other words, they say that they believe there is a God who lives in heaven, but because they have not actually seen him, they cannot know for sure that he exists. However, the Bible *never* makes a distinction between faith and knowledge. The fact that we make a distinction is a result of a misunderstanding of the two ideas.

Faith is not wishful thinking or an excited emotional state. Hebrews 11:1 says, "Now faith is being sure of what we hope for and certain of what we do not see." Being sure and certain does not involve wishful thinking and merely hoping that there is a God. It is being certain—pure and simple! It *is* knowledge! To say, "I just believe that Jesus is going to come back someday" in the same way that an abandoned, abused and forgotten child believes that his father is somehow going to return is not biblical faith. Knowing that something is going to happen before it actually does is similar to the same confidence we have that the sun is going to rise tomorrow.

Most of what we *know* has not come to us through our observing it, but is based on evidence of its existence. For example, fewer people actually saw John F. Kennedy than the number of those who know that he lived. How? On the basis of the evidence of his life. The same is true of spiritual truths that we have not physically observed. On the basis of the evidence of the life of Jesus Christ, we can know that these things he said are true and are going to happen. Furthermore, if we have to see something to know it exists, then none of us could say that we know we have a brain, for example, because we have never seen it!

Here in 5:1, Paul is saying that the crumbling and wasting away of our bodies ("earthly tents") was intended to cause us to focus on the existence of an eternal home. If we can know that eternal realities do exist by observing the creative power of our God, then the wasting away of our world, and particularly our bodies, shows us clearly that these eternal realities do not include the present world that we live in. These realities, or specifically our eternal home, cannot be "built with human hands." Humanity has nothing to with our eternal well-being. With that in mind it is much easier to denounce the world and not to be intimidated by it because of its inability to satisfy our deepest needs.

Groaning but Growing

²Meanwhile we groan, longing to be clothed with our heavenly dwelling, ³because when we are clothed, we will not be found naked. ⁴For while we are in this tent, we groan and are burdened, because we do not wish to be unclothed but to be clothed with our heavenly dwelling, so that what is mortal may be swallowed up by life.

Paul now moves into our emotional response as disciples to the reality of our human condition. Human suffering causes different reactions depending on the contents of the heart. When the storms hit, some lose heart, becoming discouraged and despondent, while others become bitter, hard and pridefully independent. Suffering in the life of a disciple of Christ, however, produces a longing for that which is eternal. Like non-Christians, "we groan and are burdened," but unlike them, suffering points us to the ultimate relief found only in heaven.

The main criticism of Christianity by the philosophers of the world is that we invented the eternal realm to give us the hope we need to endure suffering in this life. We are accused of being escapists and idealists. Instead of being strong people of character, we are accused of retreating into a world of illusion in order to avoid facing life as it is. But the Bible teaches exactly the opposite: Suffering helps us recognize the true nature of our existence.

The evidence is clear. The world is wasting away, and so are we, along with it. That is the truth. That is as empirical and objective as you can get. Human strength is no match for the reality of death, and death, in fact, is the ultimate proof of the weakness and hopelessness of humanity. Strength of character has no influence over death.

This finite process of death was never meant to cause us to stand our ground and live and act as if we were going to live forever, which is the false and fabricated idealism of the world. Dying and the pain associated with it were meant by God to open our eyes to our need for resurrection, living forever and embracing the eternal. If most people did not believe that life is worth living, why would they be willing to endure suffering? And what gives life its true worth cannot be attributed to anything having to do with the physical realm of existence. It is only those values having to do with the eternal that give us a reason for pushing through and holding on to life.

> *[5]Now it is God who has made us for this very purpose and has given us the Spirit as a deposit, guaranteeing what is to come.*

Oftentimes the complexities and trials of life are intensified by our inability to comprehend the reasons why we have been placed in this world. It is easy to say, "Well, we know God disciplines those that he loves" (see Hebrews 12), and yet, seriously doubt and fail to be joyful and secure in this process. It seems that the very nature of suffering clouds a clear look into its overall purpose.

When we suffer, our first impulse is to look for a way out of the problems in the same way we instinctively pull our hand away from a flame. Our constant avoidance of suffering hinders the whole refining process God wants it to have in our lives—let alone hindering our gratitude for the part it plays in drawing us closer to God. Paul is saying that we were created for this very purpose—in this context, to put off mortality and to put on immortality, by being transformed into the likeness of Jesus Christ. We, as God's children, must trust that there is a profound and deeply needed reason for us to be here. The intricate laws of the universe display God's incredible power to be exact, and we must trust that the same care was given to our purpose for having been brought into this world. A loving, careful and powerful God must be seen as someone given to detail, and therefore he must have a purpose for all that we experience.

Paul says that the Spirit is the deposit guaranteeing what is to come. Unfortunately, the Holy Spirit is a very mysterious and vague concept to most disciples. Because of the abuse of the teaching on the Holy Spirit in the religious world and the denominational world's use of him as a license to sin, many disciples walk on theological eggshells when approaching the topic. This hesitancy is very different from Paul's many references to the work of the Holy Spirit in his letters. We have already discussed the reference to the various aspects of the work of the Holy Spirit in 1:21-22 and do not need to repeat that discussion here. But it is important to see once again the role of the Holy Spirit in making sense of suffering in this life: He guarantees what we have coming in the next life (5:5).

As we follow Jesus Christ, we will be hard pressed, perplexed, persecuted and even struck down. We will groan and long for change. Outwardly, we may appear to be wasting away. If we only look at what is seen, we will most likely lose heart. But Paul calls us to lift up our eyes, to see that which is eternal, and to look forward to a coming glory that transforms today's troubles into petty annoyances. With such a perspective, we will believe and we will speak.

5

Always Confident and Compelled by Love

2 Corinthians 5:6-6:2

What motivated a man like Paul? Was it money? The evidence for this could hardly be less. Power? With his openness and admissions of weakness, he certainly doesn't write like a man so driven. In the passages we are about to consider, we find two keys: (1) a healthy and deep respect for God, his character and his will and (2) awe and admiration for the love of Christ that had the effect of constraining and compelling. While our cynical world may doubt that anyone can have pure motives, the Bible shows us men and women who have ambition and drive that comes from above.

One of Paul's strengths is his amazing grasp of the role of both the physical and the spiritual realms. Once our possession of eternal life becomes real to us, we can be secure spiritually as we live in the physical world. Then the physical world fulfills its purpose of causing us to put our security in the eternal relationship we have with God. This is the power of faith: We do not have to *see* everything in order to be secure that everything is under God's control. Living by sight has no trust associated with it. Faith is not only the certainty of what we can know without having to physically see it, but it also involves the resulting surrender and peace.

Living by Faith

> *5:6Therefore we are always confident and know that as
> long as we are at home in the body we are away from the
> Lord. 7We live by faith, not by sight. 8We are confident, I say,
> and would prefer to be away from the body and at home
> with the Lord.*

Being genuinely torn between living here and living
with the Lord meant that Paul believed with full confidence that after this life, he would be with the Lord. In
Philippians 1:21-25, Paul also writes,

> *For to me, to live is Christ and to die is gain. If I am to go on
> living in the body, this will mean fruitful labor for me. Yet
> what shall I choose? I do not know! I am torn between the
> two: I desire to depart and be with Christ, which is better by
> far; but it is more necessary for you that I remain in the
> body. Convinced of this, I know that I will remain, and I will
> continue with all of you for your progress and joy in the
> faith....*

This understanding gave him the needed insight into his
purpose here on earth. Paul is essentially saying that being reminded by suffering that our present home is still
here in the body also reminds us that we are away from
the Lord. The saying, "Absence makes the heart grow
fonder," relates to what Paul is saying here—in essence,
"Absence makes the heart more convinced."

> *9So we make it our goal to please him, whether we are at
> home in the body or away from it. 10For we must all appear
> before the judgment seat of Christ, that each one may re-
> ceive what is due him for the things done while in the body,
> whether good or bad.*

Most people today assume that somehow, despite the
multitude of belief systems and the various life-styles of
our world, all of us are going to end up in the same happy

place when we die. According to the teachings of Jesus, nothing could be further from the truth. It is very easy to become enraptured by the concepts associated with eternal life. The idea of life after death is captivating to both the religious and nonreligious person. With the Bible you can go as deep into this concept as you want, but no amount of study will change the fact that eternal life is found only by those who make it their goal to please God.

Paul does not leave his discussion of eternal glory out in the ozone and mystical borders of our minds. He brings it home in a very practical and sober way by referring to the "judgment seat of Christ" (5:10). This is a serious bottleneck for the many assumptions associated with the false doctrine of universal and unconditional atonement. In very practical and no uncertain terms, Paul states that it *does* make a difference how we live our lives because our lifestyle is a result of what we believe. The New Testament support of this truth is almost endless (see Matthew 5:21-30; 7:22; 10:15; 11:21-24; 12:36, 41-50; Luke 10:12-15; 11:31-54).

The fact that the world and everyone who has ever lived are moving toward a final day when all of history will come to an end is one of the central themes of the Bible. This truth is what motivated all of the great prophets and preachers of God to preach repentance. Along with the end of all history is the final separation between God's people and his enemies, between the lost and the saved (see Matthew 8:11-12.; 13:24-30; 25:31-46; Luke 16:19-31).

In the context of 2 Corinthians, the reason Paul would want to bring up the subject of the judgment seat of Christ is quite obvious. The Corinthians needed to be sobered! Though they were a relatively young congregation, they were still responsible for their attitudes and life-styles. And their abandonment and criticalness of Paul had not gone unnoticed by the Lord. This was not simply a matter between the Corinthian church and Paul over some trivial personality conflicts. They were actually being led astray by allowing false apostles to have influence over them, and they needed to realize the seriousness of their situation (see page 12). In these circumstances, a reminder of judgment is good for the soul. There is a connection between what we do now in the body and whether we will be at home with the Lord.

The Fear of the Lord

> *[11]Since, then, we know what it is to fear the Lord, we try to persuade men. What we are is plain to God, and I hope it is also plain to your conscience.*

Where does fear (5:11) fit into our motivation to serve God? Is it part of God's plan to keep us faithful until the coming of the Lord? The reality of fear in our lives is an apparent dilemma that Christians must deal with. On the one hand, the Bible teaches:

> *There is no fear in love. But perfect love drives out fear, because fear has to do with punishment. The one who fears is not made perfect in love (1 John 4:18).*

Yet, on the other hand, the Bible also teaches, "The fear of the LORD is the beginning of knowledge, but fools despise wisdom and discipline" (Proverbs 1:7). Also of note is the experience of the early church:

> *Then the church throughout Judea, Galilee and Samaria enjoyed a time of peace. It was strengthened; and encouraged by the Holy Spirit, it grew in numbers, living in the fear of the Lord (Acts 9:31).*

The question is, How can we live in the fear of the Lord, while at the same time developing perfect love, which is supposedly driving out the fear in our lives?

The Greek word, *fobos*, as is the case with most English words, can have more than one meaning. For example, in Matthew 14:26, the word is used to describe the disciples' terrified reaction to seeing Jesus coming toward them during a storm, walking on the water: "They were terrified. 'It's a ghost,' they said, and cried out in fear." However, biblically the word "fear" can refer to a healthy respect and awe of God (Psalm 19:9; Proverbs 1:7 and many others). We all have to admit that part of our motivation for becoming Christians was not only an understanding of how much God loves us but also a recognition of the seriousness and consequences of our not loving God. We felt very keenly the reality of being lost and were afraid of dying in that state—or were afraid that the Lord would come back before we had time to repent of our sins.

Many people in the denominational world react strongly against fear being used in our spiritual motivation to serve God. However, how can fear be denied? It is almost a daily reality in our lives. In fact, fear, like pain, serves a useful purpose in life. We train our children to have a right kind of fear of cars moving on a busy street or strangers who offer candy, in order to protect them and keep them from harm. The question is, *When does fear cease to serve a useful purpose and begin to be a spiritual problem?*

Obviously, it is not God's purpose for his children to *remain* in a state of being terrified (as the disciples in the boat). In Romans 8:15-16, Paul wrote:

> *For you did not receive a spirit that makes you a slave again to fear, but you received the Spirit of sonship. And by him we cry, "Abba, Father." The Spirit himself testifies with our spirit that we are God's children.*

Being a slave to fear means that we are controlled by fear. Christians now make the transition from having fear control us to a place where it helps us respect and appreciate the power and discipline of God.

Paul's use of the a father-child relationship in the Romans passage just quoted is helpful in understanding the distinction between fear and respect. A child with a controlling fear of his parents can grow up emotionally damaged and insecure. A healthy respect for the authority of his parents can be instilled in him in a very loving and secure environment. Knowing that his parents love him and want what is best for him drives out a slavish fear and implants a deep respect and appreciation for their commitment to providing him the best environment for his growth. The same is true of our relationship with God. As our love for God grows, and particularly our understanding of his love for us grows, our relationship is no longer based on fear but on a deep respect and appreciation for his plan for our lives. What we once feared—his wrath, power and ability to destroy us—matures into a respect that we can securely live under.

I like the illustration of two young boys to clarify this point. One boy had a very strong father. However, his father was strict and harsh, beating the boy regularly and unjustly. The young boy grew up in constant fear of his father, never feeling secure in his father's love for him. The other boy's father was also big and strong, yet was loving and understanding, always providing a warm environment for his son. This strength provided a strong foundation of security and protection. When the son was at school he always knew that, although his father was not physically present, if there was ever a problem, his father would be there to guide and protect him. This son grew to respect the strength of his father, admiring and imitating it for the rest of his life.

In this context, Paul is apparently reminding the Corinthians that it is his deep respect for God that keeps him working to change people's hearts and minds. Oftentimes, the phrase "we try to persuade men" (5:11) is used to stress the passion that Paul felt for lost souls—a passion he no doubt had. However, here it is being used to describe his efforts at persuading the Corinthians of the legitimacy of his ministry and life.

Out of His Mind?

12We are not trying to commend ourselves to you again, but are giving you an opportunity to take pride in us, so that you can answer those who take pride in what is seen rather than in what is in the heart. 13If we are out of our mind, it is for the sake of God; if we are in our right mind, it is for you.

Paul's primary appeal here is to how God is viewing him. To God, the issues are not complicated, but very plain. Paul's life was under the control of God, and the course of his life was being directed by the movement of the Holy Spirit, and not by Paul's own decisions. When Paul planned certain things, they first had to meet the approval of the Lord. What the Corinthians were viewing as inconsistency and fickleness, Paul viewed as simply *surrender* to the ultimate will of God. Paul does not want to be perceived here as bragging about himself, but he wants to be admired because of his commitment, hoping that the Corinthians would take a great deal of pride in Paul rather than being critical of him.

Paul's appeal to the Corinthian church throughout the letter is for them to look at life's circumstances from a spiritual point of view, not a worldly one. If we evaluate one another simply in a worldly, physical way, there is nothing much to take pride in. The decisions that Paul felt compelled to make might have made him appear to be out of his mind. However, from a spiritual point of view these decisions were the most reasonable thing to do. Anyone committed to living for God will be viewed by the world as out of his mind. The world cannot comprehend the basic idea of dying to self for the benefit of others. For example, the Roman governor Festus accused Paul of being out of his mind and insane (Acts 26:24), and Jesus himself was certainly not viewed by the people of his day with much credibility. His own family thought he was crazy (Mark 3:21), and he ended up dying alone on the cross after claiming that he was the Son of God. This level of sacrifice finds its credibility only when viewed as having been done out of principle or for the sake of others. The phrase "it is for you" (5:13) shows that all of what the Corinthians viewed as inconsistency was a result of Paul's love and sacrifice for them!

Compelled by Christ

> *[14]For Christ's love compels us, because we are convinced that one died for all, and therefore all died. [15]And he died for all, that those who live should no longer live for themselves but for him who died for them and was raised again.*

The love of Christ was the primary motivation behind Paul's ministry (5:14), which makes it senseless to accuse him of living a life of self-centeredness and selfishness. A true understanding of Christ's love is unable to produce anything but a life of selfless and sacrificial love for others. The claim of understanding the love of Christ must be followed by this type of life. A real conviction that Jesus died produces a willingness to also die. Beyond the purpose of securing the forgiveness of our sins, the practical purpose and power of the cross is to help us carry our own cross daily—to live and die as Jesus did.

Some in the denominational world would argue that this verse teaches universal, unconditional salvation for all mankind because of the phrase "therefore all died"

(5:14). But Paul is writing to disciples, so this interpretation is a definite separation of the verse from its context
and, for that matter, the context of the whole of the New
Testament. The death of Christ is incapable of producing
a life of crucified living without the involvement of our
own personal decision. Christianity is not a magic show.
What activates the power of the cross is our personal decision to embrace it. Confusion over this issue persists
because many times in the Bible, the emphasis is given to
God's work in our salvation rather than to our own response. It is easy to understand the reason for this when
you see the entire plan of God's salvation throughout history. Our decisions in the process pale in comparison to
the decisions that God has had to make and the commit-
ments that he has had to keep.

Notice Paul's words in Galatians 2:20:

> *I have been crucified with Christ and I no longer live, but
> Christ lives in me. The life I live in the body, I live by faith in
> the Son of God, who loved me and gave himself for me.*

The action of being crucified with Christ is, in one sense,
accomplished for us. This is also seen in one of the classic
passages on baptism and the cross, Romans 6:3-4:

> *Or don't you know that all of us who were baptized into
> Christ Jesus were baptized into his death? We were there-
> fore buried with him through baptism into death in order
> that, just as Christ was raised from the dead through the
> glory of the Father, we too may live a new life.*

Again, the emphasis here is on the results of being
baptized, which are being accomplished *by God* on our
behalf. Many in the denominational world have errone-
ously understood baptism to be man's work, rather than
seeing baptism as the work of God. However, it is obvious from the teachings of the Bible that Jesus' death on

the cross did not automatically produce salvation for every person, only *the possibility* of that salvation. The fact that God does the saving does not negate our responsibility to respond correctly to his work. In Acts 2:38 Peter clears up the problem when he says,

> *"Repent and be baptized, every one of you, in the name of Jesus Christ for the forgiveness of your sins. And you will receive the gift of the Holy Spirit."*

Our repentance is necessary for baptism to have any effect on our sinful nature. The death of Christ should never be used to alleviate the commitment we have made and the godly pressure we need to feel in order to live lives that are pleasing to God. The incredible love that was displayed when Jesus died on the cross for each one of us gives us the reason, and thus the motivation, not to give up.

A New Creation

> [16]*So from now on we regard no one from a worldly point of view. Though we once regarded Christ in this way, we do so no longer.* [17]*Therefore, if anyone is in Christ, he is a new creation; the old has gone, the new has come!*

There should be little doubt where Paul is going with his argument: The cross not only gives us freedom from our sins but also from our former way of thinking. Disciples evaluate reality in a completely different way than the world does. The Corinthians' view of Paul had turned worldly in that they were viewing Paul in the same way that the Jews had viewed Jesus. Paul himself had once been extremely critical of Jesus, the most spiritually perfect man who ever lived. His mind was blinded by his own self-righteousness and legalism, and he became full of critical and negative thinking. Yet, Paul's conversion to Christ had opened his eyes and allowed him to possess and to enter a whole new world of love, spirituality, insight and freedom.

How we think and view life plays such a crucial role in our ability to endure trials and our ability to capture the necessary vision to fuel our spiritual longevity. Viewing one another according to the flesh is no longer a part of our lives. Because of the death, burial and resurrection of Christ, there is now a new way to look at one another and to live together. The existence of the church in Corinth was a result of the transformation of the worldview of Paul. Under his old way of thinking, he would never have had a vision for a city like Corinth, full of Gentiles and pagans. His legalism and self-righteousness as a Pharisee would have kept him from seeing the potential for such a city—in the same way that Jesus' disciples failed to see the potential for a town like Sychar in Samaria (see John 4).

On a more practical level, it is important to realize that being a new creation and feeling like a new creation are two different things. Often young disciples expect that the powerful feelings of newness at the time of their baptism are going to last forever. It does not take long to realize that feelings are feelings, which means they will come and go. That is the basic nature of feelings. After baptism is when the real battle begins. Learning that you are a sinner while studying to become a Christian is vastly different than confronting your sin on a daily basis after baptism. That confrontation is seldom filled with exhilarating emotional highs. In fact, seeing our weaknesses can be very discouraging. Yet, because of the grace of God, none of this changes the fact that we are new creations. This is the exciting part of the battle and all the more reason to stay in it. The old way of life is gone—giving into sin and being controlled by our feelings. The new life has come—confronting our sin and battling it on a daily basis.

Reconcilable Differences

> [18]*All this is from God, who reconciled us to himself through Christ and gave us the ministry of reconciliation:* [19]*that God was reconciling the world to himself in Christ, not counting men's sins against them. And he has committed to us the message of reconciliation.*

The word "reconciliation" (5:18) is a crucial word. It not only resolves the problem of a world separated from God and people separated from one another, but also takes care of the immediate and practical problem between Paul and the Corinthians. Reconciliation resolves everything. *Webster's* says that to reconcile is "to restore to friendship or harmony; to settle, resolve."

God is unquestionably the source of the reconciliation in our relationship with him, and his passion and commitment to each of us should convict us of our need to be united and resolved in our relationships with one another. It is very easy to get a bit bogged down in the "theology" of reconciliation and lose our emotional contact with the heart of God. Studying closely the history of Israel helps us see his heart for his people. The many times and ways that God has kept his commitment to the nation of Israel during trying times is moving and challenging.

One excellent example of God's undying commitment to his people is found in the message of the prophet Hosea. Hosea was called by God to marry an adulterous woman and from that experience to preach and convey the feelings of God to his people. Hosea not only felt the agony of adultery, but after his wife, Gomer, left and sold herself into poverty and slavery, he went to buy her back in an attempt to reconcile the relationship. Hosea's life was a message to Israel.

Also God made the promise to Abraham that he would make him into a great nation and bless all nations through his seed—his seed, of course, being the Christ. That promise carried God through hundreds and thousands of years of spiritual adultery from the Israelites, and each time God forgave them and held firm to his promise. The plan of reconciliation must produce the same commitment in every disciple.

Paul further says, "And he has committed to us the message of reconciliation" (5:19). The "us" does not seem to be referring to all disciples, even though it certainly has some application. But here the emphasis is on Paul and his companions. He has been specifically and purposefully selected as one of God's apostles to carry God's message to the Gentile world. A "message of reconciliation" implies that there is a messenger, and if the messenger is ignored, so is the message. Paul is making it clear that by criticizing him, the Corinthians were not just rejecting a man but the very plan of God for the world.

Ambassadors of God

> [20]*We are therefore Christ's ambassadors, as though God were making his appeal through us. We implore you on Christ's behalf: Be reconciled to God.* [21]*God made him who had no sin to be sin for us, so that in him we might become the righteousness of God.*

An ambassador is someone who is sent in the name of someone else. An ambassador is more than just a messenger but is responsible for representing the convictions and views of the one he is representing. An ambassador for a king is obligated to accurately represent the beliefs and convictions of the king and his country. Paul is using the same imagery to clarify his responsibility to Christ.

It is beyond our ability in this life to comprehend why God chose to make his appeal through sinful men, especially in that it is easy to imagine other ways he could have chosen to communicate to the world—through angelic beings or his own voice, etc. Yet, we must remember that the essence of the message of reconciliation is salvation. Reconciliation is an experience, in this case, resulting in salvation. In one sense we do not qualify as God's ambassadors, being imperfect yet representing a perfect God. But on the other hand, we qualify incredibly because we have experienced the results of being reconciled to God through grace!

Despite some positive developments in Corinth, Paul's admonition to "be reconciled to God" (5:20) definitely indicates the serious spiritual state of the Corinthian church, or at least some of those within the church. If Paul was, as he claimed, an ambassador of Christ through whom God was making his appeal, the Corinthians had essentially placed themselves in the same situation as those who rejected the Old Testament prophets. Jesus said in the Sermon on the Mount,

> *"Blessed are you when people insult you, persecute you and falsely say all kinds of evil against you because of me. Rejoice and be glad, because great is your reward in heaven, for in the same way they persecuted the prophets who were before you" (Matthew 5:11-12).*

2 Corinthians 5:21 has received a great deal of attention throughout the years by Bible scholars and theologians because of the sentence, "He made him who knew no sin to be sin on our behalf" (NASB). Exactly what does "he made him...to be sin" mean? Was Jesus made to be a sinner? Other places in the Bible it is clear that Jesus was sinless. Hebrews 4:15 says,

> *For we do not have a high priest who is unable to sympathize with our weaknesses, but we have one who has been tempted in every way, just as we are—yet was without sin.*

1 John 3:5 expresses the same idea: "But you know that he appeared so that he might take away our sins. And in

him is no sin." And yet here, Paul writes, "God made him...
to be sin."

The reason this verse is so controversial is because of
the importance of Jesus remaining sinless in order to secure our salvation. The book of Hebrews shows clearly
the connection between the sacrificial system of the Jews
and the sacrifice of the Christ: The whole purpose for the
animal sacrifices in Judaism was to point to the need for
a more effective way of removing sins. Part of that system was the sacrifice of an unblemished lamb to take on
the sins (blemishes) of the whole nation. Therefore, the
sacrifice of Jesus had to be a perfect sacrifice: "the righteous for the unrighteous, to bring you to God" (1 Peter
3:18). Hebrews 9:14 emphasizes the same point:

> *How much more, then, will the blood of Christ, who through
> the eternal Spirit offered himself unblemished to God, cleanse
> our consciences from acts that lead to death, so that we may
> serve the living God!*

The idea of God making Jesus to be sin is undoubtedly
parallel to the rituals connected to the Day of Atonement
recorded in Leviticus 16. On that day certain prescribed
animal sacrifices were made to remove the sins of the
people of Israel. Animals were sacrificed, and the blood
was used to consecrate both the people and the various
objects connected with the Most Holy Place, where God's
presence dwelt. A live goat was spared and set aside for
another aspect of the removal of the nation's sins which
is described in Leviticus 16:20-22:

> *"When Aaron has finished making atonement for the Most
> Holy Place, the Tent of Meeting and the altar, he shall bring
> forward the live goat. He is to lay both hands on the head of
> the live goat and confess over it all the wickedness and re-
> bellion of the Israelites—all their sins—and put them on the
> goat's head. He shall send the goat away into the desert in*

the care of a man appointed for the task. The goat will carry
on itself all their sins to a solitary place; and the man shall
release it in the desert."

This goat has traditionally come to be known as the *scapegoat*. In other words, all of the sins of the people were placed on the goat, and the goat then carried the sins outside of the camp. Obviously, this act was symbolic. Sin always involves a transgression of God's will. The goat *carried* sin but was not *guilty* of sin. This is true also in the case of Jesus. As God placed the sins of a nation on the head of a goat, so he places our sins on the head of his son. Jesus was not made a sinner in a literal sense, but he carried our sins to the cross. (See Isaiah 53:10 and Galatians 3:13-14.)

The Time of God's Favor

6:1As God's fellow workers we urge you not to receive God's grace in vain. 2For he says,

"In the time of my favor I heard you,
    and in the day of salvation I helped you."

I tell you, now is the time of God's favor, now is the day of salvation.

One of the most extraordinary themes in the Bible is the mercy and grace of God. Grace is typically defined as "unmerited favor." We have been given eternal life without the requirement of having to qualify for it. Motivated out of his love for the Corinthians, it is clear that Paul is trying his best to deal with the Corinthians as sensitively and gently as possible in order to persuade them to repent. God had truly placed the Corinthians in an atmosphere of forgiveness and mercy.

Yet, the purpose for God's mercy and grace is always repentance. In dealing with some of the hypocrisy among those with a Jewish background in the church in Rome, Paul wrote:

> *Or do you show contempt for the riches of his kindness, tolerance and patience, not realizing that God's kindness leads you toward repentance? (Romans 2:4).*

He later wrote to Titus:

> *For the grace of God that brings salvation has appeared to all men. It teaches us to say "No" to ungodliness and worldly passions, and to live self-controlled, upright and godly lives in this present age (Titus 2:11-12).*

If there is no repentance, then the grace of God has been received in vain. Sooner or later, we have to face the Lord. If what he has done for us is not producing a humility leading to repentance, then we are essentially saying that what he has done is not powerful enough or significant enough to produce any kind of change in our lives.

Paul quotes Isaiah 49:8 (6:2) to further emphasize his point. This passage was originally used to convey God's mercy in bringing the Israelites out of captivity and restoring them once again in the promised land. That is always the purpose of God: reconciliation. The time had come for the Corinthians to hear his voice and recognize the importance and seriousness of the salvation of the Lord.

In the upcoming text Paul will work hard to solidify his relationship with the Corinthian disciples. He will succeed in his mission if they will believe that his motivation is of the highest variety, and if they will join him in knowing the fear of the Lord, being compelled by the love of Christ and believing that today is the day to accept God's grace and the changes it brings.

6
Open Wide Your Hearts

2 Corinthians 6:3-7:16

Though his relationship with the Corinthian church was severely strained at times, Paul never gave up on God's power to bring changes to their lives. In the following passages we find Paul calling for a greater openness on their part (after he has re-opened his heart to them), but we also hear him rejoicing over some progress he had heard that they had made. These verses about Paul, about the Corinthians and about their interaction are rich with insights that can make major differences in our lives and our own ministries:

> *6:3We put no stumbling block in anyone's path, so that our ministry will not be discredited. 4Rather, as servants of God we commend ourselves in every way: in great endurance; in troubles, hardships and distresses; 5in beatings, imprisonments and riots; in hard work, sleepless nights and hunger; 6in purity, understanding, patience and kindness; in the Holy Spirit and in sincere love; 7in truthful speech and in the power of God; with weapons of righteousness in the right hand and in the left....*

One of the crucial concerns in Paul's life was the removal of stumbling blocks from the lives of his brothers and sisters. A "stumbling block" in this case (6:3) may have been any example that caused a brother or sister to sin. In most cases these involved an issue of opinion, or as Paul describes them in Romans 14:1, "disputable matters." There are many things that we, as disciples, are free to do. However, exercising that freedom might cause other disciples to struggle in their faith. Paul said in 1 Corinthians 8:9, "Be careful, however, that the exercise of your freedom does not become a stumbling block to the weak."

Paul is taking this principle, which in other contexts he has applied to only disputable issues, and is applying it to his total way of life. We should be impressed with the lengths to which Paul was willing to go to fulfill the responsibilities of his ministry. He was cautious earlier to avoid the accusation of self-commendation, when he says, "Are we beginning to commend ourselves again?" (3:1a) Here in 2 Corinthians 6, he basically allows his life to speak for itself:

> ...*8through glory and dishonor, bad report and good report; genuine, yet regarded as impostors; 9known, yet regarded as unknown; dying, and yet we live on; beaten, and yet not killed; 10sorrowful, yet always rejoicing; poor, yet making many rich; having nothing, and yet possessing everything.*

All of the spiritual attributes that Paul had previously mentioned (6:4-6) had produced opposite reactions. At times his life-style had brought him great glory. Other times, it had brought him great dishonor. Even though his experiences proved the genuineness of his motives, he was still labeled as an impostor. The opposite was also true. Even though he appeared as if he was going to die, he lived on. Even though there were times of great sorrow, in reality he was always rejoicing. With this passage Paul is relating back to the theme of "the smell of death" introduced in 2:16. His ministry appeared one way to the world and quite another way to God. The Corinthians were again forced to decide how they were going to view him. Were they going to dishonor him while he was at the same time receiving the glory of God? Would they call him an impostor while his motives were being judged as genuine in heaven?

Setting the Pace

> *[11]We have spoken freely to you, Corinthians, and opened wide our hearts to you. [12]We are not withholding our affection from you, but you are withholding yours from us. [13]As a fair exchange—I speak as to my children—open wide your hearts also.*

One thing is abundantly clear: Paul has been amazingly, and even courageously, open with the Corinthians about his life, his motives and his love for his spiritual children. The courage of such openness becomes obvious when we recognize how critical many of the Corinthians had become of Paul and how hard it must have been to be open in the presence of such criticalness. It takes a great deal of humility in such situations to be open and to continue to love when the response is unloving and disloyal.

Yet, openness is always powerful and convicting, and if the listener has a heart that is seeking God, openness always has an impact. This was Paul's conviction. Even though the Corinthians had so much to deal with and to struggle through, Paul had confidence that deep inside there was a love for God and for righteousness. If the Corinthians would simply imitate Paul and open their hearts, allowing their feelings for Paul to once again be brought to life, then there would be hope for a new beginning in their relationship.

Be Holy

> *[14]Do not be yoked together with unbelievers. For what do righteousness and wickedness have in common? Or what fellowship can light have with darkness? [15]What harmony is there between Christ and Belial? What does a believer have in common with an unbeliever? [16a]What agreement is there between the temple of God and idols?*

The passage beginning in 6:14 and continuing through 7:1 has been a topic of discussion among many scholars.

Some feel that the verses are out of context with the pre-
ceding and following thoughts. For example, 6:13 ends
with "open wide your hearts also." Then we have a break
in thought until 7:2, "Make room for us in your hearts." In
between the issues dealing with the heart, there is the
idea of not being yoked together with unbelievers. Some
scholars propose that this section was later interjected,
or that it was part of another letter of Paul's later added
to 2 Corinthians, or even that it was never written by Paul
and added later by the early church. However, these theories go beyond the evidence.

Paul uses the word "unbeliever" here to make his point.
The only other place that he uses this word is in 4:4 where
he writes:

> *The god of this age has blinded the minds of unbelievers, so
> that they cannot see the light of the gospel of the glory of
> Christ, who is the image of God.*

In looking at the whole context of 2 Corinthians, one
of Paul's primary purposes for writing the book was to
deal with the "false apostles" (11:13), who were corrupt-
ing and influencing the Corinthians. It is more than likely
that the term "unbeliever" in 4:4 was being used to describe these false teachers. If that is the case, after appealing to the Corinthians to open wide their hearts to
him in 6:13, Paul then begins to deal with the reason they
had not opened their hearts, which had to do with their
relationship with the false teachers. After dealing with
this Paul returns to his plea in 7:2, to "make room for us
in your hearts." In other words, there is no real problem
with the content, if we allow Paul to build it according to
his purposes.

Many scholars fail to recognize that a shift in thought
does not necessarily mean a change in context. Also, from

the author's point of view, context is very subjective and relative. Each author determines his own context, and, quite frankly, context is not a serious consideration in writing from an author's point of view. He simply writes to make his point. Now, on the other hand, from the reader's point of view, context is very important in order to find out what the author's point is. In that respect, things must be kept in context.

Now let's look at the meaning of the passage (6:14-16). The imagery is two oxen in the field yoked together. The point is that where one goes, the other has to go. Paul is not using this illustration because he is confident that the Christian will always control the direction of the non-Christian. If that were true, it would be great to be yoked with an unbeliever! Paul is concerned because the opposite is usually the case.

Christians who allow themselves into close (and usually unspiritual) relationships with non-Christians are usually the ones led into sin or back into the world. Paul made it clear in 1 Corinthians 5:9-10 that disciples cannot shun the world, implying the need to be in relationships with people of the world. In fact, making disciples of all nations demands that we learn how to build spiritual friendships with non-Christians. However, there is a point in relationships when a dangerous yoke develops between two people. Things go beyond the needed trust and friendship of a normal relationship and begin to take on a stronger than normal influence of one person over the other. In some relationships, this is expected; for example, the Christian marriage relationship and parent-child relationship. However, in other relationships it becomes a serious spiritual problem when the convictions of the unbeliever begin to influence and weaken the convictions of the believer.

In 6:14b-16, Paul asks several rhetorical questions using obvious opposites to make his point. There are some things in this world that do not and cannot, by their very nature, belong together. Where one exists, the other cannot. The presence of light always means an end to darkness. Righteousness interacts with wickedness in the same way. The classic standoff in this passage, of course, is between Christ and Belial. ("Belial" is most likely a reference to the devil.) There is no greater spiritual contradiction or wider fixed chasm than that which exists between Christ and the devil. There is no hope of reconciliation, negotiation, fellowship or even the slightest chance of a remote friendship. This law of opposites must always be recognized by disciples in the realm of human relationships.

As disciples of Christ it is imperative to our well-being spiritually to become comfortable with these principles. There are just some things in this world that are absolutely incompatible with the Christian life. One of the sad characteristics of the world is that it is always in a constant process of change, and not for the better. Therefore, Christians never have the luxury of blending in, hiding or going unnoticed. The incompatibility of the world with the kingdom of God will always keep that from happening. That we as God's people are able to see the "light of the gospel of the glory of Christ" should make us grateful that the chasm between the light and darkness is so absolute.

Purity Supreme

16b For we are the temple of the living God. As God has said: "I will live with them and walk among them, and I will be their God, and they will be my people."

*17 "Therefore come out from them
    and be separate,
        says the Lord.*

> Touch no unclean thing,
>   and I will receive you."
>   ¹⁸"I will be a Father to you,
>   and you will be my sons and daughters,"
>   says the Lord Almighty.
>
> ^{7:1}Since we have these promises, dear friends, let us pur-
> ify ourselves from everything that contaminates body and
> spirit, perfecting holiness out of reverence for God.

Paul says that our being "the temple" of the Lord (6:16b) is reason for living a holy and separate life. Though the idea of a temple does little to stir our emotions today, in the first century it was a very real and moving illustration. Paul most assuredly did not have in mind a Greek temple, such as the temple dedicated to the worship of Aphrodite in Corinth. Greek temples were not places known for their holiness and spiritual devotion! Paul had in mind the temple of the Lord located in Jerusalem, which for centuries was revered as the dwelling place of the Lord. The temple was steeped in the tradition of the Jews and spiritually protected by all types of purification rites. For example, the high priest was allowed to enter the Most Holy Place of the temple, the actual place where the presence of God was found, only once a year, and only after he had purified himself from his sins. The ordinary Jew was never allowed to enter such a place representing the holiness of God.

Paul first described the church collectively as the temple in 1 Corinthians 3:16 and now reminds these same believers of it again (6:16b). Disciples represent the temple of the Lord, the dwelling place of God, because he lives in the church through his Spirit—in contrast to living in a building. Notice Paul's words in 1 Corinthians 3:16: "Don't you know that you yourselves are God's temple and that God's Spirit lives in you?"

Jesus said, "If anyone loves me, he will obey my teaching. My Father will love him, and we will come to him and make our home with him" (John 14:23). The fact that God lives in us should motivate us to keep ourselves spiritually pure and righteous, just as we would prepare our personal home for a special guest. Our welcome mat for the Lord is a pure and righteous life.

The passages that Paul quotes from the Old Testament to give authority to his admonition (6:16c-18) all contain the call to holiness, followed by the promise of a relationship with God. The first citation, found in Leviticus 26:12, is surrounded by some of the most incredible promises found in the Old Testament. Yet, before the promises could be fulfilled, the Israelites were told to prove their devotion to the Lord by obedience. Second, Isaiah 52:11 emphasizes the need to be separate and to touch no unclean thing. In the old law, there were hundreds of laws dealing with how to stay "ceremonially clean"—that is, approved for worship. When a Jew came in contact with something that was considered unclean, there was always something that he could do to purify himself. It was usually something external and physical, but the challenge of purity under the new covenant is now a matter of the heart. Jesus said,

> *"What comes out of a man is what makes him 'unclean.' For from within, out of men's hearts, come evil thoughts, sexual immorality, theft, murder, adultery, greed, malice, deceit, lewdness, envy, slander, arrogance and folly. All these evils come from inside and make a man 'unclean'"* (Mark 7:20-23).

Third, Paul uses 2 Samuel 7:14 (6:18) to show the special relationship of family that God desires to have with us. The verse was originally spoken by the prophet Nathan about Solomon, who was to build a temple to God. The inspired apostle adds "and daughters" to the verse, as if to be sure to include the sisters in the call to repentance and to receive the resulting promises of God.

These extraordinary promises (6:16b-18) demand the right response. Focusing on the promises of God (7:1) is one of the most exciting adventures of the Christian life. Understanding what we have in Christ changes our view of repentance. Repentance was never meant to be negative, but refreshing (Acts 3:19). Being separate from the world was always meant by God, our Father, to be a homecoming to his dwelling.

With His Heart on His Sleeve

> *²Make room for us in your hearts. We have wronged no one, we have corrupted no one, we have exploited no one. ³I do not say this to condemn you; I have said before that you have such a place in our hearts that we would live or die with you. ⁴I have great confidence in you; I take great pride in you. I am greatly encouraged; in all our troubles my joy knows no bounds.*

Paul now returns to the theme of the heart. In 6:13 Paul pleaded for the Corinthians to open their hearts to him. Now again, he asks the same thing. Spiritual reconciliation and unity is an issue of the heart. Jesus never demanded that his disciples be sinless, yet when we become critical and legalistic in our hearts, we begin to expect perfection from one another. It becomes hard to forgive and to see past each other's imperfections. Many parents, for example, are able to look past the imperfections of their children. Why? Because of their intense love for and loyalty to their children. Paul is simply asking for the same consideration.

Jesus never demanded that his disciples be perfect in the sense of being sinless (see 1 John 2:1-2). He does call us to seek his heart. There is a big difference. Jesus said,

> *"'Love the Lord your God with all your heart and with all your soul and with all your mind.' This is the first and greatest commandment"* (Matthew 22:37-38).

Even in the midst of all of our imperfections, there is still the opportunity for a close and intimate relationship with God. The same is true in our relationships with each other. How can we expect perfection from one another when our own personal lives are so full of sin? Only when we are able to see beyond the flesh and into each other's hearts do we have any hope for real unity. If only the Corinthians could see Paul's commitment to them. If only they could see the willingness in his heart to *live or die* with them, his great confidence in them, his great pride in them and his boundless joy about his relationship with them, things would have been very different in the church—and ultimately in the great city of Corinth.

How Good Is a Timely Word!

> *⁵For when we came into Macedonia, this body of ours had no rest, but we were harassed at every turn—conflicts on the outside, fears within. ⁶But God, who comforts the downcast, comforted us by the coming of Titus, ⁷and not only by his coming but also by the comfort you had given him. He told us about your longing for me, your deep sorrow, your ardent concern for me, so that my joy was greater than ever.*

We have already discussed that the reason that Paul was not able to keep his word and visit the Corinthians was because of the intensity of the situation in Macedonia. Paul was being tested on every level: spiritually, emotionally and physically. We would think that when Paul speaks of being comforted or of God being the "God of all comfort" (1:3), he would be speaking in terms of a change in his circumstances or an end to the sufferings. Yet, as we can see here, that was not the case. It was simply hearing about the Corinthians' longing, concern, deep sorrow and joy for him that made Paul feel comforted.

This passage (7:5-7) provides us with some of the greatest insight into Paul's heart and into what it means to love the ministry. That there were signs of the

Corinthians beginning to turn their hearts back to Paul was, to him, the greatest treasure of all—even beyond the removal of the actual sufferings and hardships, and his own personal comfort. The hope he had for the Corinthian church to change was obviously a key to Paul's endurance and the reason for the intensity of his efforts towards them. Even as bleak as the situation still was in Corinth, to him, their emerging repentance was well worth all of his sacrifice, hard work and his weathering of all the personal attacks against him.

Sorrowful As God Intended

> *⁸Even if I caused you sorrow by my letter, I do not regret it. Though I did regret it—I see that my letter hurt you, but only for a little while—⁹yet now I am happy, not because you were made sorry, but because your sorrow led you to repentance. For you became sorrowful as God intended and so were not harmed in any way by us.*

We must always believe that the confrontation of sin will have a positive result. This takes faith in God and in the power of his Word. When Paul wrote his first letter confronting the Corinthians' sin, there was no guarantee of what their response would be. Paul had no way of knowing how extensive the sin was in Corinth or how much the false teachers had influenced the congregation. All he knew for sure was that his letter would produce a reaction and that initially, the Corinthians would be hurt by it.

Sentimentality (meaning here, allowing our emotions to cause a softening of God's standard) is one of the greatest problems in the church. It is often mistaken for love and is therefore tolerated without realizing how deadly its existence can be. The spiritual life of whole religious movements, denominations and churches have been choked out by its lethal influence. Sentimentality stands for nothing and puts up with everything. The greatest temptation that Paul probably felt in all of his struggles with the Corinthians was to *not* write to confront their sin, saving himself the pain of a negative reaction. Sentimentality is not focused on what is best for those around us but is self-focused and is self-protective. The reality that Paul mentioned in 4:5, "For we do not preach ourselves, but Jesus Christ as Lord," must apply in our closest and most intimate relationships.

Paul wrote in Ephesians 4:15, "Instead, speaking the truth in love, we will in all things grow up into him who is the Head, that is, Christ." In order for spiritual growth to take place three things need to be present: (1) love, (2) truth and (3) speech. True love means that we want what is best for each other, which in the kingdom of God is becoming more like Christ and growing spiritually. Love provides the hope, vision and encouragement necessary to do that. Becoming like Christ is impossible without the truth. Where are we spiritually? What are our weaknesses? How do we overcome and win the victory over our sinful nature? The truth was designed to set us free (John 8:31-32). Speech is none other than a loving person getting the truth into someone else's life. All of these are essential to making disciples. These three realities characterized Paul's relationship with the Corinthians.

Times of Refreshing

[10]*Godly sorrow brings repentance that leads to salvation and leaves no regret, but worldly sorrow brings death. *[11]*See what this godly sorrow has produced in you: what earnestness, what eagerness to clear yourselves, what indignation, what alarm, what longing, what concern, what readiness to see justice done. At every point you have proved yourselves to be innocent in this matter. *[12]*So even though I wrote to you, it was not on account of the one who did the wrong or of the injured party, but rather that before God you could see for yourselves how devoted to us you are.*

The rewards for confronting and dealing with sin are found in the repentance that it produces. Here Paul makes an important distinction that will help us in bringing others to repentance—understanding the distinction between godly and worldly sorrow. Distinguishing between the two is vital in that one leads to salvation and the other leads to death. The difference is in the fruit: Godly sorrow produces repentance, and worldly sorrow does not.

Worldly sorrow (7:10) is deceptive because it produces many of the same responses as godly sorrow—admission of sin, tears and feelings of guilt. Yet, the difference is significant enough to result in either life or death. Worldly sorrow is never able to completely free the sinner of regret. Even when there is a glimpse of hope for repentance, the sinner's regret over having to leave the sin and the world chokes out the conviction needed to produce genuine repentance.

Godly sorrow is not difficult to achieve. We must simply have the willingness to let God bring us deep conviction. Neither is it difficult to detect in the lives of others. It is not, as some religious people teach, a very private and personal dynamic between the individual and the Lord. On the contrary, earnestness, eagerness, indignation, alarm, longing, concern and readiness to see justice done (7:11) are all clear evidence that godly sorrow exists in the heart. These characteristics are not hidden! In fact, it is impossible to keep them secret. There is no secret discipleship being taught here. Godly sorrow is an obvious response of which worldly sorrow is not even a close imitation.

The last part of this passage (7:12) may seem a bit inconsistent with Paul's purposes in this letter. But he is not negating the fact that he wrote to deal with those who were causing trouble in Corinth, to those who were doing the wrong and to those who had been wronged. The overall purpose was, however, to show the Corinthians that deep within their hearts there was still a love and loyalty for him. The repentance that had taken place was an obvious sign that the Corinthians were not too far gone.

Righteous Boasting

[13]By all this we are encouraged.

In addition to our own encouragement, we were especially delighted to see how happy Titus was, because his spirit has been refreshed by all of you. [14]I had boasted to him about you, and you have not embarrassed me. But just as everything we said to you was true, so our boasting about you to Titus has proved to be true as well. [15]And his affection for you is all the greater when he remembers that you were all obedient, receiving him with fear and trembling. [16]I am glad I can have complete confidence in you.

Paul has a special gift of pulling his readers in emotionally. There are many challenging passages in this letter where Paul speaks forthrightly and directly to the Corinthians. However, at the same time, chapter 7 is perhaps the warmest and most encouraging section of any of Paul's letters. Phrases such as "my joy was greater than ever," "we were especially delighted" and "I am glad I can have complete confidence in you" show the emotions that were on Paul's heart. Some of us would have difficulty expressing ourselves in the latter way to a church like the one in Corinth. Yet, despite of all of the problems, Paul was able to have hope and confidence. Effective ministry always emerges out of the balance between a tough love and a deep emotional tie with those we disciple. Here Paul has given us some of the most useful principles for ministry and human relationships found anywhere in the Bible.

This entire section is a powerful reminder that those of us who have God's Spirit and great promises can resolve the toughest relationship challenges. We can be convicted of sin, experience godly sorrow and go on to the refreshment of repentance. We can also speak the truth in love and help others to come to a humble change of heart. Paul was a man who allowed God to bring conviction to his own heart, which paved the way for him to speak truthful and healing words to others. We must learn from both his experience and that of the Corinthians.

7
Sacrificial Giving

2 Corinthians 8 and 9

In 2 Corinthians 8 and 9 Paul turns his attention to a specific matter in the Corinthian church that he wanted to bring to completion, but in so doing he teaches disciples in all generations some powerful lessons about what he will call "the grace of giving." It seems obvious from New Testament evidence that Paul is dealing in this context with a collection for the poor Christians in Jerusalem. In 1 Corinthians 16:1-4, Paul had previously admonished the Corinthians to set aside some money on the first day of every week to be collected when Paul arrived. Paul was then going to send some men to Jerusalem to deliver the money. But then, as now, people had to be inspired and motivated. They had to see the connection between their giving, their hearts and their faith. To follow Jesus Christ is to become a generous giver. This Paul makes clear.

Eagerly Remembering the Poor

8:1And now, brothers, we want you to know about the grace that God has given the Macedonian churches. 2Out of the most severe trial, their overflowing joy and their extreme poverty welled up in rich generosity. 3For I testify that they gave as much as they were able, and even beyond their ability. Entirely on their own, 4they urgently pleaded with us for the privilege of sharing in this service to the saints.

Acts 2:41 shows us that 3,000 people were baptized to begin the church in Jerusalem, and later we know that the number of disciples grew to 5,000 men (Acts 4:4). Acts 2:44-45 says,

All the believers were together and had everything in com-
mon. Selling their possessions and goods, they gave to any-
one as he had need.

With the church growing so rapidly, along with the immense economic problems these young converts faced, the church undoubtedly faced serious financial challenges. Philip Hughes, in his commentary on 2 Corinthians, states:

> The material cost to the majority of this great num-
> ber must have been immense. Coming as they did from
> the background of Jewish fervor and exclusivism, it
> needs no demonstration that they must have become,
> in consequence of their conversion, the victims of so-
> cial and economic ostracism, ecclesiastical excommu-
> nication, and national disinheritance. Their business
> enterprises must in most cases have collapsed in ruins
> and family bonds been heart-breakingly severed.[1]

Paul had already been involved in helping in a relief ef-fort to Jerusalem, which is recorded in Acts 11:27-30:

> *During this time some prophets came down from Jerusa-*
> *lem to Antioch. One of them, named Agabus, stood up and*
> *through the Spirit predicted that a severe famine would*
> *spread over the entire Roman world. (This happened during*
> *the reign of Claudius.) The disciples, each according to his*
> *ability, decided to provide help for the brothers living in*
> *Judea. This they did, sending their gift to the elders by*
> *Barnabas and Saul.*

Due to Paul's change of plans in not visiting the Corinthians (1 Corinthians 16:5-9), he was not able to send the collection on to Jerusalem. Therefore he takes up the matter again here in 2 Corinthians. Due to the sensitivity of the relationship between Paul and the Corinthians and their continued criticism of him, he approaches the issue of money somewhat cautiously, but also skillfully. There is a lot to learn here on how to best get a desired response from a sticky situation.

Paul begins by calling the opportunity to give, the "grace" of giving (8:7). One of his main examples is the churches in Macedonia. We need to remember that the situation in Macedonia was the main reason Paul had not yet been able to visit the Corinthians. He is now able to use his time with the Macedonians as a means of moving the hearts of the Corinthians. Preaching on the topic of giving to people struggling with trust and critical attitudes would probably be viewed by them as somewhat manipulative—certainly not as an opportunity. The response of the Macedonians, however, is undeniable and above criticism.

Paul was able to see in the Macedonians what was seemingly impossible. The Macedonians were living through "the most severe trial" and in what Paul describes as "extreme poverty" (8:2). Yet, there was "overflowing joy...rich generosity," a giving "beyond their ability" and an urgent pleading for the "privilege of sharing in this service to the saints." This is an amazing response possible only when disciples truly view giving as a "grace." It is no wonder that Paul begins with their example in order to show clearly the kind of response he was expecting from the Corinthians.

The Call to Excellence

> *[5]And they did not do as we expected, but they gave themselves first to the Lord and then to us in keeping with God's will. [6]So we urged Titus, since he had earlier made a beginning, to bring also to completion this act of grace on your part. [7]But just as you excel in everything—in faith, in speech, in knowledge, in complete earnestness and in your love for us—see that you also excel in this grace of giving.*

The achievement of anything great in the kingdom of God begins with an intense devotion to the Lord. To give joyfully in the midst of extreme poverty can only be accomplished by a close walk with God. The Lord is the wellspring and source of all we are able to accomplish spiritually. He is able to open our eyes to see beyond what we can see physically in order to grasp the immense, unseen spiritual blessings we have in Christ. A true understanding of what we have in Christ enables us to give up all that is wasting away and earthly. Jesus said, "But seek first his kingdom and his righteousness, and all these things [food, drink and clothing] will be given to you as well" (Matthew 6:33). The Macedonians were a demonstration of the reliability of that promise.

Giving ourselves to the Lord always necessitates that we will give ourselves to one another—the body of Christ. This is God's will. In 1 Corinthians 1:10-12, Paul describes the division that was taking place in the church in Corinth. Though there was the claim by the disciples in Corinth that they were following the great leaders God had given them, in reality they were dividing and destroying the unity that they had once experienced. All of this was done in the name of God and supposedly for his purpose. The Macedonians, on the other hand, out of their devotion to God, were becoming more devoted to Paul and to his ministry, wholeheartedly supporting this cause that was so close to his heart. There should be little doubt that Paul is not only citing the example of the Macedonians to convict the Corinthians in the area of giving, but also to help them see their lack of support and respect for Paul.

Paul mentions bringing to completion the giving and later admonishes the Corinthians to "finish the work" (8:11). This, of course, implies at least an initial commitment to the plan. Because of the extenuating circumstances of Paul's missionary plans, their giving was interrupted but now needed to be resumed. The challenge Paul gives the Corinthians is not only to give, but to give excellently. He places giving on the same level as faith, speech, knowledge, complete earnestness and love. Oftentimes we put giving in its own category, rather than recognizing the spirituality involved in sacrificial giving. God expects excellence in this area of spiritual living as in all other areas of Christian living. This involves not only the amount or percentage of our income when we give, but also the attitude and heart behind our giving.

The Ultimate Example

> *[8]I am not commanding you, but I want to test the sincerity of your love by comparing it with the earnestness of others. [9]For you know the grace of our Lord Jesus Christ, that though he was rich, yet for your sakes he became poor, so that you through his poverty might become rich.*

The phrase "I am not commanding you" (8:8) is a difficult passage to explain, especially after Paul admonishes the Corinthians to excel in the area of giving and to finish the work that they had started. Why is Paul not wanting to command them? Looking deeper to find the answer to this question will provide us some valuable insight into Paul's method of motivating the Corinthians toward sacrificial living. In chapters 8 and 9 Paul is not dealing with a collection for missionary or administrative purposes. He has in mind a collection for the poor. However, the principles he is teaching have a practical application to every type of giving. It is important to accept what Paul is saying here and trust that his overall methodology in the end is very powerful and effective.

Paul makes it clear that he intends "to test the sincerity" (8:8) of the Corinthians' love for the Lord by comparing their reaction to the reaction of the Macedonians and also to the example of Jesus Christ himself. In many nations of the world poverty is something that most of the general population has absolutely no control over. In

America and other first world countries, the individual can usually better his financial situation, while in other countries, people are born into the financial situation in which they will remain their entire lives. In either case, few people willingly live in poverty if they can avoid it. The reluctance to give sacrificially may be seen as a result of an instinctive fear of being impoverished. Paul introduces Jesus as an example of someone who willingly embraced poverty out of his love and commitment to make others rich. The example of Jesus is the essence of sacrificial giving and is Paul's goal for the hearts of the Corinthians.

As a leader, often it is easier and more efficient to simply command something to take place instead of trusting in the power of love and the power of example to bring about the results. Though Paul understood that some things needed to be dealt with by way of command (1 Timothy 1:3), some things are, in fact, hindered from happening by commands. Commanding someone to do something is not the only—or always the most effective—way to get something accomplished. Commanding someone to give very rarely produces sacrificial giving. It might produce giving, but it will rarely be sacrificial. Inspiring and convicting people by using the example of others, as well as challenging them on the sincerity of their love, has a much better chance of producing the quality of giving exemplified by Jesus himself.

A Matter of Heart

> [10]And here is my advice about what is best for you in this matter: Last year you were the first not only to give but also to have the desire to do so. [11]Now finish the work, so that your eager willingness to do it may be matched by your completion of it, according to your means. [12]For if the willingness is there, the gift is acceptable according to what one has, not according to what he does not have.

Again, Paul's approach to the issue of giving is seen in his use of the word "advice" (8:10). Yet, his plan is clearly spelled out by referring to what is best for the Corinthians. Even though he refers to himself as *advising* them, his original readers are left with the haunting question: How can people seeking to be sacrificial refuse what is best? He reminds them of their prior commitment, complimenting them that they were the first to both give and to have the desire to give. It is on the basis of this prior commitment that Paul challenges them to finish the work.

The area of money is always a sensitive area to deal with because of abuses of finances in the religious world and because people's hearts get so tied to their finances. Many leaders feel awkward having to constantly bring to the church's attention the importance of meeting a budget. But every disciple needs to have the conviction to do his part in making sure the financial obligations of the church are met. If every disciple would simply fulfill the responsibility to give sacrificially in supporting the work of the Lord, there would not be the problem that often exists in many churches. An eager willingness means nothing without the completion of the decision. And in many cases it is easy to *feel* like we are eager and willing to do something, but the real test of our eagerness is whether or not we *do* what we promised we would.

Paul stresses that our gifts are acceptable only on the basis of what we have (8:12). Giving beyond what we have is not ours to give and is therefore not sacrificial. Though giving beyond our ability is sometimes done out of a immature sincerity, it is often an indication of trying to impress other people or meeting the goals that other people have for us. People-pleasing is abhorrent to God (Matthew 6:2-4). God wants our giving to be a reflection of our love for him, and it was never intended to elevate us in the opinion of others or to cause us to go into debt.

What Goes Around Comes Around

> *[13]Our desire is not that others might be relieved while you are hard pressed, but that there might be equality. [14]At the present time your plenty will supply what they need, so that in turn their plenty will supply what you need. Then there will be equality, [15]as it is written: "He who gathered much did not have too much, and he who gathered little did not have too little."*

The point of our giving is "that there might be equality" (8:13). It was the conviction of the early disciples that it was their personal responsibility to take care of each other. This meant nothing other than sacrificial giving because of the tremendous challenge to take care of all of the new converts that had come from all over the world for the celebration of Pentecost. "All the believers were together and had everything in common. Selling their possessions and goods, they gave to anyone as he had need" (Acts 2:44-45).

Paul uses Exodus 16:18 to make his point about equality (8:15), but he is probably pointing to the wider context of the overall problem the Israelites were having with greed. During their wilderness experience, the Israelites were totally dependent on God to provide them with the basic necessities of life. Food and water in the barren desert had to come directly from God. Each day God sent them a food substance which the Israelites called "manna," and they were told to collect it each day, but only enough to last through the day. Everybody was given what they needed, and if any was left over, it would rot before the coming of the next day. This forced the Israelites into a daily dependence on God and an equality, not allowing anyone the opportunity to stockpile any of the available resources. This required the Israelites to focus on the needs of others, which is the essence of sacrificial giving.

Love in Action

> [16]*I thank God, who put into the heart of Titus the same concern I have for you.* [17]*For Titus not only welcomed our appeal, but he is coming to you with much enthusiasm and on his own initiative.*

Titus played a significant role in Paul's relationship with the Corinthians. He was mentioned several times throughout this letter (2:13; 7:6, 13, 14; 8:6, 16, 17, 23; 12:18). These references indicate that Titus was Paul's emissary and probably the mediator between him and the Corinthians. It is obvious that his presence was pivotal in that he brought good news about the Corinthians to Paul and returned to them with news and directives from Paul. Paul is careful to point out that Titus was more than just a go-between, but was enthusiastic—and even initiated the trip out of his own eagerness to visit the Corinthians. A messenger is not always well received and is seldom very useful in resolving conflict unless he has some emotional connection with the situation. This was not a political situation that could be resolved by a detached ambassador, but was a family situation requiring an emotional commitment of each person to bring about resolution.

Righteous Before Men

> [18]*And we are sending along with him the brother who is praised by all the churches for his service to the gospel.* [19]*What is more, he was chosen by the churches to accompany us as we carry the offering, which we administer in order to honor the Lord himself and to show our eagerness to help.* [20]*We want to avoid any criticism of the way we administer this liberal gift.* [21]*For we are taking pains to do what is right, not only in the eyes of the Lord but also in the eyes of men.*
>
> [22]*In addition, we are sending with them our brother who has often proved to us in many ways that he is zealous, and now even more so because of his great confidence in you.* [23]*As for Titus, he is my partner and fellow worker among you; as for our brothers, they are representatives of the*

churches and an honor to Christ. [24]Therefore show these men
the proof of your love and the reason for our pride in you, so
that the churches can see it.

It is impossible to know who "the brother" that Paul
referred to was. There have been a multitude of possibilities set forth such as Luke, Barnabas, Silas, Timothy,
Aristarchus (Acts 19:29) and so on. Acts 20:4 mentions
several other brothers traveling with Paul on his way to
Macedonia, who are also possibilities. On the other hand,
it could have been a brother that we know nothing about.
Amazingly, scholars throughout history have devoted a
fair amount of time to setting forth their various opinions
on this rather minor detail.

Who the unnamed brother was is not as important
as *what* he was. He was obviously held in high regard
and respected throughout several churches, which
showed their collective trust for the plan to take the collection to Jerusalem. I might be reading a bit too much
between the lines, but in light of the tension between
Paul and the Corinthians, it seems that the need for es-
corts might be a result of the lack of trust in the relationships. It would seem that if Paul was behind the plan
and was taking on the responsibility of seeing that the
money got to Jerusalem, that would have been enough.
We do know from 1 Corinthians 9 that there were some
issues having to do with Paul not being supported by the
Corinthians, which shows a serious lack of trust on their
part. On the other hand, the journey to Jerusalem was a
long and, in many ways, dangerous trip, which might
have demanded a traveling party to ensure that the
money arrived safely.

Preparing to Be Generous

[9:1]*There is no need for me to write to you about this ser-*
vice to the saints. [2]For I know your eagerness to help, and I

have been boasting about it to the Macedonians, telling them
that since last year you in Achaia were ready to give; and
your enthusiasm has stirred most of them to action. ³But I am
sending the brothers in order that our boasting about you in
this matter should not prove hollow, but that you may be ready,
as I said you would be. ⁴For if any Macedonians come with
me and find you unprepared, we—not to say anything about
you—would be ashamed of having been so confident.

We need to notice how Paul used the power of example to inspire sacrificial giving. At the beginning of chapter 8, he used the examples of the Macedonians and Jesus himself to show the Corinthians the meaning of sacrificial giving. Here he has turned the tables. He mentioned in 8:10 that the previous year, the Corinthians were the first not only to give, but to have the desire to do so. What is amazing is that Macedonian churches' exceptional generosity was in part motivated by the original desire of the Corinthians to give! Then the resulting gifts were used by Paul to remotivate the Corinthians.

Paul mentions twice that he had boasted about the willingness of the Corinthians to help the situation in Jerusalem (9:2-3). It is clear here that Paul, after doing so much boasting about the Corinthians, did not want to be embarrassed or caught off guard at the unreadiness of the Corinthians. It would have made for an awkward situation for both Paul and the Corinthian church. This is the reason initially that Paul had asked the Corinthians to lay aside a certain amount each Lord's day, so that when he arrived, there would not have to be a collection taken up (1 Corinthians 16:1-4).

A Lesson from Agriculture

⁵So I thought it necessary to urge the brothers to visit you in
advance and finish the arrangements for the generous gift
you had promised. Then it will be ready as a generous gift,
not as one grudgingly given.

> *⁶Remember this: Whoever sows sparingly will also reap sparingly, and whoever sows generously will also reap generously. ⁷Each man should give what he has decided in his heart to give, not reluctantly or under compulsion, for God loves a cheerful giver.*

In this passage we find great insight into the reason for Paul's methodology, as well as wisdom on how to achieve sacrificial giving in our own hearts. Paul makes an important contrast between a generous gift and one grudgingly given. One is not only given out of generosity, but is also generous in the amount. The opposite is true of a grudgingly given gift. Because of the reluctance, the amount is always going to be lower than something given out of appreciation.

Due to the nature of the times, many of the illustrations found in the New Testament come from the agricultural world. Paul introduces the idea of sowing and reaping in order to make a significant point about giving (9:6). The whole purpose behind the energy and sacrifice of sowing is the expectation that there will be a harvest or the opportunity to reap from what was sown. The amount reaped is always proportional to the amount that was sown. No one can expect to reap much if the sowing was only minimum in amount or in effort. The same is true in the spiritual realm. There is always a connection between the sowing and the reaping. Notice what Paul says in regard to the spiritual life in general:

> *Do not be deceived: God cannot be mocked. A man reaps what he sows. The one who sows to please his sinful nature, from that nature will reap destruction; the one who sows to please the Spirit, from the Spirit will reap eternal life. Let us not become weary in doing good, for at the proper time we will reap a harvest if we do not give up (Galatians 6:7-9).*

What is obvious here is that in any realm, be it giving or personal spiritual growth, generous sowing always produces generous reaping.

Paul stresses the need for the giver to decide for himself the exact amount to be given: "Each man should give what he has decided in his heart to give, not reluctantly or under compulsion, for God loves a cheerful giver" (9:7) Why is it important for the giver to make his or her own decision? Reluctance is the greatest threat to generous giving. The words "reluctance" and "compulsion" are dependent to some degree on context for their definitions here. Paul intended for each disciple to determine the amount that he or she would give. When that is not allowed to happen, then reluctance and compulsion come into play. In the same way, a cheerful giver is also defined by the context. When the *personal decision* of the giver is denied, then, according to this context, Paul does not consider him a cheerful giver.

There is no doubt that Paul believed in persuading others to give. In fact, it is obvious that his goal for the Corinthians is for them to be sacrificial givers. However, in trying to persuade the Corinthians to give sacrificially, part of Paul's strategy is to recognize the important relationship between freedom and motivation. A heart without freedom (or one feeling under compulsion) will never give sacrificially. The level of sacrifice that Paul is referring to, that is, of the Macedonians and Jesus himself, is impossible to achieve with reluctance in the heart. A reluctant person holds back. A cheerful giver is the only one with any hope of imitating Jesus in sacrifice.

Paul used the examples of the Macedonians and Jesus to create more faith and joy in the hearts of the Corinthians, because it is the joy and faith in the heart of each disciple that determines whether sacrificial giving occurs. A heart full of joy and faith will always give more than a heart that is under "command," which is why the amount given was ultimately left to the decision of each individual.

Divine Care

> [8]And God is able to make all grace abound to you, so that in all things at all times, having all that you need, you will abound in every good work. [9]As it is written:
>
> "He has scattered abroad his gifts to the poor;
>   his righteousness endures forever."
>
> [10]Now he who supplies seed to the sower and bread for food will also supply and increase your store of seed and will enlarge the harvest of your righteousness. [11]You will be made rich in every way so that you can be generous on every occasion, and through us your generosity will result in thanksgiving to God.

Sacrificial giving is an issue of faith. This is the challenge of Paul's analogy between giving and sowing. A farmer, because of his experience and knowledge of the laws of nature, is able to trust that if he sows generously and is able to control the water and sunlight supply, he will reap a great harvest. The challenge in the area of giving is to have the same faith and confidence that God is going to work in our lives financially to take care of us.

Our confidence in how God works must be as strong as our confidence in the laws of nature. No one in their right mind questions whether the sun will rise tomorrow or that sometime today it is going to get dark. The spiritual laws established by God are just as true. In the same way that God is the source behind the order and growth in the natural and physical world, so is he the source of all that we have financially. And sacrificial givers have always been taken care of by God.

An amazing thing to notice is that God is the source of both the seed and the harvest. We often think that if God would only give us the opportunity, then we could do the rest: "If only he would give me the job that I need, then I would make the money." "If only God would bring me an open person, then I would be able to bear fruit." In other words, we want the seed from God, and then we want to take credit for the harvest. But, God provides both!

> *Every good and perfect gift is from above, coming down from the Father of the heavenly lights, who does not change like shifting shadows (James 1:17).*

In 9:9 Paul quotes from Psalm 112:9 to add authority to the point he is making. Psalm 112 shows the link between trusting in the Lord, righteousness and prosperity. The first two sentences of Psalm 112:9 seem to connect giving to the poor with the endurance of our righteousness. However, the wider context shows that the main point of the psalm is trusting in God, which then enables us to give freely to the poor and in turn adds to the longevity of our righteousness. Paul is using this reference to show that the idea of being made "rich in every way" (9:11) is not just financial wealth. Multiplication of righteousness is another result of trusting God, which is the reason Paul refers to "the harvest of your righteousness" (9:10). When righteousness and faith are present, sacrificial giving is not far behind. Such giving in turn brings an even greater harvest of righteousness.

A Shining Example

> [12]*This service that you perform is not only supplying the needs of God's people but is also overflowing in many expressions of thanks to God. [13]Because of the service by which you have proved yourselves, men will praise God for the obedience that accompanies your confession of the gospel*

*of Christ, and for your generosity in sharing with them and
with everyone else. [14]And in their prayers for you their hearts
will go out to you, because of the surpassing grace God has
given you. [15]Thanks be to God for his indescribable gift!*

What Paul wants to see happen is far beyond a mere collection for the poor brothers and sisters in Jerusalem, as important as that was. The need of the hour in Corinth was the development of disciples with rich and generous hearts, grateful to God for all that he had done for them. Though the physical needs of the poor disciples would be alleviated, God was going to be glorified by the many more expressions of thanks given to him because of the Corinthians' generosity. Also, there was going to be a deeper bond between the European churches and the church in Jerusalem. This gift that Paul was on his way to pick up had immeasurable potential in both the physical and spiritual realms. It was going to meet the physical needs of the Christians, as well as produce within both the givers and the recipients valuable spiritual results. "Thanks be to God for his indescribable gift!" (9:15).

We are never more like God and his Son Jesus Christ than when we are giving. If our hearts have not become generous, we have little understanding of the message of the cross or the grace of God. Someone has written, "All our theology must eventually become biography. The constant challenge of this life we call Christian is the transition of all we believe to be true into our day-to-day lifestyle."[2] This is what Paul is calling for in the lives of the Corinthians. God wants them—and us—to live what we believe, and to give as he gives. Jesus' words recorded only in Acts 20:35 say it clearly: "'It is more blessed to give than to receive.'"

8
Dealing with False Apostles

2 Corinthians 10

It is obvious from the change in Paul's tone that he is feeling a lot at this point in his writing. He had spent considerable time and energy, as well as a lot of patience, in dealing sensitively with the Corinthians in the attempt to help them come to a full and lasting repentance. However, now the time had come to deal with those who were refusing to repent and who were the main cause of the problems. Paul's accusers had focused on Paul's weaknesses and the softness of his demeanor. Now they were going to have to deal with Paul's directness and the power of his rebuke. This transition in tone in no way reflects an inconsistency in Paul's leadership, but rather, the balance one needs to be an effective leader. There was no one more gentle than Jesus Christ, but when it was time to be direct, as recorded in Matthew 23, there was no one more powerful.

Chapter 10 marks a definite transition in Paul's thought and tone and has caused scholars to raise questions about this part of the letter. Those wanting to examine these questions more closely can find more information in the back of this book.[1]

Quite a Reputation

> [10:1]*By the meekness and gentleness of Christ, I appeal to you—I, Paul, who am "timid" when face to face with you, but "bold" when away! [2]I beg you that when I come I may not have to be as bold as I expect to be toward some people who think that we live by the standards of this world.*

The contents of chapters 10 and 11 do, in fact, deal with the overall theme of this letter. Paul is now turning his attention to the false teachers in the congregation who have negatively influenced the Corinthians. The "I, Paul," of 10:1 cannot be ignored. The false teachers were keeping with their pattern of accusing Paul of fickleness and inconsistency of character. Paul was basically a humble and gentle man, as disciples must be. If the situation warranted, he could have come across much stronger. Some of the Corinthians were interpreting his humility and gentleness as timidity. When Paul wrote to the Corinthians in order to deal with sin in the church, as in 1 Corinthians, he was accused of harshness while he was away from them. Yet apparently, some in Corinth were accusing him of timidity while he was with them. They seemed to have been accusing him of keeping something back and not being straightforward and honest. Their other accusation, as previously discussed, was that he was inconsistent, and therefore, unreliable. Both assertions fit well into the false teachers' purposes of undermining Paul and winning the Corinthians over to themselves.

Paul answers his accusers with the proper blend of both gentleness and strength. First, he appeals to the gentleness and meekness of Christ. How can anyone claiming to be a disciple argue against that? It is *not* a weakness to be meek—it is a strength. Second, he appeals to how he will be, if necessary, when he arrives in Corinth. In fact, he hopes that he will not have to be as bold as it seems the Corinthians want him to be. Paul makes it clear that he is not going to be reduced to the standards of the world, but that he is going to conduct himself according to spiritual principles and not worldly ones (10:2).

Fight the Good Fight

> *³For though we live in the world, we do not wage war as the world does. ⁴The weapons we fight with are not the weapons of the world. On the contrary, they have divine power to demolish strongholds. ⁵We demolish arguments and every pretension that sets itself up against the knowledge of God, and we take captive every thought to make it obedient to Christ.*

Paul uses the analogy of warfare to make his point about the battle between the physical world and the spiritual realm. It must be understood that the spiritual man and the worldly man are going to use different weapons in war—not only because of the effectiveness of the various weapons, but also because of the different goals and purposes of the two armies. This truth is nowhere clearer than when Jesus stood before his accusers at his trial. He said virtually nothing. To the world he looked weak and defeated. We would have loved to see him in a masterful oratory of cutting logic and argumentation or in a never-before-seen display of supernatural power with thousands upon thousands of angels standing by his side, anticipating the signal to attack. That is the worldly side of us. The spiritual side must trust in the power of silence and humility, recognizing their supremacy over the weapons of the world. Hate often seems more powerful than love and has an immediate satisfaction that is alluring and tempting. But in the end, hate is always defeated by the power of love. The false teachers in Corinth would have loved nothing more than for Paul to get down on their level and engage in battle. To argue and hate and fight for an arrogant supremacy was a battle they had been thoroughly trained for, and they were therefore battle-ready. Paul refused the invitation.

By refusing, Paul was not raising the white flag of surrender. In fact, victory was absolutely a part of his agenda.

The difference between him and the false teachers was the location of the battle and the strategy for victory. For the false teachers, their pride was at stake: Who would have the most influence over the Corinthians—Paul or them? They were thinking primarily about themselves. To Paul, the battle was not about him but about the souls of his spiritual children, the Corinthians. Spiritual weapons would ensure Paul of the victory.

Paul's battle was definitely a battle for the mind. He sets forth a powerful illustration of demolishing the walls of an ancient fortress or stronghold and taking prisoners, forcing them into submission and obedience. The parallel is the fortress we let Satan build around our minds and hearts, and his prisoners are our sinful thoughts and convictions. The purpose of the army of Christ is to penetrate these fortresses and lead out the prisoners and make them captive and obedient to Christ. In this case Paul was specifically saying that the wisdom from God would destroy the arguments and claims of the false apostles and bring about an exaltation of Christ, but the principle here is far-reaching. With spiritual weapons we can destroy false reasoning, whether the battleground is our own mind or some academic or theological arena.

Justice Will Be Served

> *[6]And we will be ready to punish every act of disobedience, once your obedience is complete.*

Whatever the Corinthians had come to believe about the character of Paul, he was now making clear what his real intentions were. He was ready to do battle, not in the ways of the world, but by the spiritual principles the Holy Spirit had revealed to him. He had formerly written in 1 Corinthians 4:19-21,

> *But I will come to you very soon, if the Lord is willing, and*
> *then I will find out not only how these arrogant people are*
> *talking, but what power they have. For the kingdom of God*
> *is not a matter of talk but of power. What do you prefer?*
> *Shall I come to you with a whip, or in love and with a gentle*
> *spirit?*

The offers still stands in 2 Corinthians. Paul was not afraid to confront the arrogant ones because he was confident that he was sent by God and that God would take care of them—and him.

Paul makes an important distinction between the whole church at Corinth and those who were causing problems. This distinction allows him to acknowledge the godly sorrow of the congregation in 7:9b-13, while also dealing with the false teaching and influence of the few throughout the letter, particularly in chapters 10 and 11. This is a very effective way of addressing the church with an admonishing, hopeful spirit while at the same time letting the condemnation of those who oppose him be known to all. When referring to the false teachers, he addresses them only in the third person, signifying to them that they were not even considered significant enough to deal with directly. He assumes here that the obedience of the Corinthians will be complete and also assumes that there will be some who will not have repented who will need to be punished.

A Shallow View

> [7]*You are looking only on the surface of things. If anyone*
> *is confident that he belongs to Christ, he should consider*
> *again that we belong to Christ just as much as he.*

"Belonging to Christ" is not a matter of the flesh, outward appearance or worldly talent, but is of the Spirit and is only spiritually discerned and attained. Paul had made it clear in 1 Corinthians that the message of the cross is foolishness to the world—something only spiritually discerned and appreciated (1:18). True unity and brotherhood is not attained by measuring each other in an arrogant, critical and unspiritual way. It comes only by acknowledging each other as being in the family of God. The sense of pride we have of being in a particular family forces us to acknowledge the importance and need we have for the other family members. Family means there are others besides us who define it. The reality of belonging to Christ must produce a deeper loyalty to one another than even to our biological relationships.

Appointed by God

[8]For even if I boast somewhat freely about the authority the Lord gave us for building you up rather than pulling you down, I will not be ashamed of it.

Developing the right perspective about authority is one of the great challenges of being a disciple of Jesus Christ. Most of denominational "Christianity" does not have to deal with this challenge, because it teaches a Christianity that is without authority—which is no true Christianity at all. Though denominationalism might hold theoretically that the existence of God and the Bible implies an authority, in practical terms these churches deny any real need for authority. But the biggest challenge associated with authority has nothing to do with acknowledging an abstract, universal standard of some kind, but rather with acknowledging the human vessels to whom God has given authority in his family. This was the problem in Corinth: They refused to recognize Paul as someone to whom God had given authority.

Like every human institution, the church has a necessary authority structure in order for it to fulfill its purpose. The challenge is that this authority takes on human form—

flesh and blood. God puts people over us in order to help us grow and become solid Christians of deep conviction and character. One of the most notable passages on this topic is found in Hebrews 13:17:

> *Obey your leaders and submit to their authority. They keep watch over you as men who must give an account. Obey them so that their work will be a joy, not a burden, for that would be of no advantage to you.*

Three words, "obey," "leaders" and "submit" pretty well sum up the main issues surrounding authority. Authority has been instituted by God and the only proper response to it is obedience and submission. (This, of course, implies that the authority we are under is consistent with the ultimate authority we have in God and in the Bible.) Paul was appointed by God to be an apostle in order to help the church mature and grow. Ephesians 4:11-13 teaches,

> *It was he who gave some to be apostles, some to be prophets, some to be evangelists, and some to be pastors and teachers, to prepare God's people for works of service, so that the body of Christ may be built up until we all reach unity in the faith and in the knowledge of the Son of God and become mature, attaining to the whole measure of the fullness of Christ.*

The purpose of Paul's authority was to help the Corinthians to grow. God had placed him in their lives as a father (1 Corinthians 4:15), and just as a father uses his authority to nurture and raise his children, so was Paul given the same responsibility and privilege. The lack of trust on the part of the Corinthians had reduced the relationship to one of authority and obedience. Paul was not reluctant about this responsibility, and just as a loving father will assert his authority or discipline his children for their good, Paul was willing to do the same.

No Duplicity

> [9]*I do not want to seem to be trying to frighten you with my letters. [10]For some say, "His letters are weighty and force-ful, but in person he is unimpressive and his speaking amounts to nothing." [11]Such people should realize that what we are in our letters when we are absent, we will be in our actions when we are present.*

Paul is here (10:9-11) elaborating on the same accusations he had mentioned in 10:1. His accusers were constantly trying to show the inconsistencies of his life. They said he was one thing in his letters and someone else in person. Paul wanted it to be known that when he arrives, there will not be a difference at all. If the false teachers thought him to be powerful in his letters, then they can expect the same when he arrives.

A Workman Approved

> [12]*We do not dare to classify or compare ourselves with some who commend themselves. When they measure themselves by themselves and compare themselves with themselves, they are not wise. [13]We, however, will not boast beyond proper limits, but will confine our boasting to the field God has assigned to us, a field that reaches even to you. [14]We are not going too far in our boasting, as would be the case if we had not come to you, for we did get as far as you with the gospel of Christ. [15]Neither do we go beyond our limits by boasting of work done by others. Our hope is that, as your faith continues to grow, our area of activity among you will greatly expand, [16]so that we can preach the gospel in the regions beyond you. For we do not want to boast about work already done in another man's territory. [17]But, "Let him who boasts boast in the Lord." [18]For it is not the one who commends himself who is approved, but the one whom the Lord commends.*

Paul is being a bit facetious here as he shows the futility of self-commendation. There is no way to convince somebody of that if he always considers himself right. Self-commendation is a way to ensure that we will always be right in our own eyes. How can we ever go wrong if we ourselves are always the standard? The only problem is that we will never be wise except in our own eyes!

Paul introduced God into the situation as a better standard when he mentioned the mission field that God had assigned to him—which included the Corinthians (10:13-14). The issue here is that Paul is not claiming any authority for himself but is only fulfilling the responsibility that had been given to him. God had assigned him the responsibility of the Corinthians and it was only in that respect that he could he boast in his work. The only ones who are to be commended are the ones that the Lord himself commends.

Jeremiah, whom Paul quotes, made the point well when he said,

> *"Let not the wise man boast of his wisdom*
> *or the strong man boast of his strength*
> *or the rich man boast of his riches,*
> *but let him who boasts boast about this:*
> *that he understands and knows me,*
> *that I am the LORD, who exercises kindness,*
> *justice and righteousness on earth,*
> *for in these I delight,"*
> *declares the LORD (Jeremiah 9:23-24).*

Paul had many things from a worldly perspective that he could have boasted in, but he learned, as did Jeremiah, through his experience of walking with the Lord, that the only real possession in life worth boasting about was his relationship with God. All other valuable attainments were merely a result of that relationship and were therefore to God's glory.

9

Are They Servants of Christ?

2 Corinthians 11

Now we come to what has to be one of the more interesting chapters in all the Bible and one that in a real way underlines the major message of 2 Corinthians—that is, that God works through our humanity. Paul, the inspired apostle, is also Paul *the man* in an awkward position. He wants to bring the Corinthians back into full fellowship and unity with him, but their reaction to him and their acceptance of his critics have put him on the horns of dilemma. He does not want to boast about himself, but he does want to set the record straight. The result is a vigorous defense of his life and ministry and then a candid admission that really the only thing we can boast about are the things that show our weakness.

Turnabout Is Fair Play

> *11:1I hope you will put up with a little of my foolishness; but you are already doing that. 2I am jealous for you with a godly jealousy. I promised you to one husband, to Christ, so that I might present you as a pure virgin to him.*

Though Paul has shown the futility of self-commendation, the Corinthians were obviously impressed by this sort of persuasion to some extent, so he now uses the tactics of his opponents. His motives, however, are totally different. His purpose is not to build himself up in their eyes, but to win back their hearts and to show them that he can match even the self-commending methodology of the false teachers.

The jealousy (11:2) that Paul felt was not for his own sense of greatness, but jealousy a father would feel for his daughter. His purpose was to present her (the Corinthians) as a pure virgin to the bridegroom, Christ. Here, we can again see the tremendous responsibility that Paul felt for the mission field that God had given him. The seriousness of the Corinthians' spiritual situation is reflected in the comparison Paul makes to the potential of presenting someone to Christ sexually impure. This type of imagery makes it clear why Paul felt the emotions that he did, and why he was fighting so hard for the hearts of the Corinthians. One of the most admirable qualities that we see here in Paul's life is how he cared for the spiritual well-being of those around him. Any defense of himself in 2 Corinthians is not for his personal self-glorification but to preserve the relationship between himself and the Corinthians, which they so desperately needed.

Be on Guard!

> *3But I am afraid that just as Eve was deceived by the serpent's cunning, your minds may somehow be led astray from your sincere and pure devotion to Christ.*

Paul moves from the example of a virgin being presented to her husband to the deception of Eve and the consequent Fall of Man. This is the strongest reference Paul has made so far to the influence of the false teachers on the church. Even though the Corinthians were responsible for *allowing* themselves to be deceived, the false teachers were responsible for their cunning, manipulative, deceptive and Satanic persuasion. The image we get of Satan and his tactics from Genesis 3 shows his incredible deceitfulness and total opposition to God.

Satan's main weapon is the lie, and he wields it powerfully and effectively. Paul had said earlier in this letter

that "the god of this age has blinded the minds of unbelievers, so that they cannot see the light of the gospel of
the glory of Christ, who is the image of God" (4:4). Jesus
referred to Satan as "the father of lies" and even said that
"there is no truth in him" (both, John 8:44). This is not a
pretty picture of Satan and, likewise, of the false teachers
in Corinth.

Paul wants to make it clear that the Corinthians' original loyalty to him was a result of their "sincere and pure
devotion to Christ" (11:3). Not only were the Corinthians
jeopardizing their relationship with Paul, they were, by
doing so, jeopardizing their relationship with Christ. The
way back to Christ in this situation was through their relationship with Paul because, as the apostle John taught
in 1 John 4:20-21:

> *If anyone says, "I love God," yet hates his brother, he is a
> liar. For anyone who does not love his brother, whom he has
> seen, cannot love God, whom he has not seen. And he has
> given us this command: Whoever loves God must also love
> his brother.*

The Corinthians' lack of love for Paul clearly signified their
lack of love for God.

The Gospel or *No* Gospel

> *⁴For if someone comes to you and preaches a Jesus other
> than the Jesus we preached, or if you receive a different spirit
> from the one you received, or a different gospel from the one
> you accepted, you put up with it easily enough.*

The issues between Paul and the church could not be
viewed as simple personality conflicts or two different
ways of looking at the same thing. The pure and simple
reason for the problems in Corinth was because a different Jesus and gospel were being preached. This language
is very similar to what Paul told the churches in Galatia:

> *I am astonished that you are so quickly deserting the one*
> *who called you by the grace of Christ and are turning to a*
> *different gospel—which is really no gospel at all. Evidently*
> *some people are throwing you into confusion and are trying*
> *to pervert the gospel of Christ (Galatians 1:6-7).*

As suggested earlier, it seems likely that the doc-
trines of the false teachers in Corinth were similar, or
even identical to, the false teachings that were pervert-
ing the churches in Galatia. It is hard to know for sure
what these teachings were, but the contrast Paul makes
between the old and new covenants in 3:6-18 is along
the same lines as what he does in Galatians 3:22-29.
Paul's tone in 2 Corinthians seems a bit gentler (if referring to the false teachers as "Satan" can be called
gentler!) compared to his powerful condemnation of
the teachers in Galatians 1:8:

> *But even if we or an angel from heaven should preach a*
> *gospel other than the one we preached to you, let him be*
> *eternally condemned!*

Whether or not the false teaching in Corinth was the
same as what was being taught in Galatia, both were producing the same fruit—a critical and disloyal attitude toward Paul. We have already seen the critical attitude here
in 2 Corinthians, and it can also be seen concerning the
Galatian situation in Galatians 4:15-17:

> *What has happened to all your joy? I can testify that, if you*
> *could have done so, you would have torn out your eyes and*
> *given them to me. Have I now become your enemy by telling*
> *you the truth?*
> *Those people are zealous to win you over, but for no good.*
> *What they want is to alienate you from us, so that you may*
> *be zealous for them.*

Egos Run Amuck

> [5]*But I do not think I am in the least inferior to those "super-apostles."* [6]*I may not be a trained speaker, but I do have knowledge. We have made this perfectly clear to you in every way.*

The facetiousness of Paul continues with his reference to the "super-apostles." These teachers were anything but super in Paul's mind, but he is referring to them by what they were claiming to be. It is obvious from Paul's correspondence that much of the criticism he was receiving revolved around his public speaking and appearance. In 1 Corinthians 2:1, Paul said,

> When I came to you, brothers, I did not come with eloquence or superior wisdom as I proclaimed to you the testimony about God.

In 10:10 of 2 Corinthians, as we already pointed out, Paul quotes his critics as saying,

> For some say, "His letters are weighty and forceful, but in person he is unimpressive and his speaking amounts to nothing."

The world puts great stock in outward appearance and persuasive eloquence. In the first-century Greek world of which Corinth was a part, eloquent public speaking was a very respected achievement—much more than it is today. Greek philosophers spent a great amount of time perfecting their ability to capture the admiration of their listeners with their eloquent oratory. Admittedly, strengths in these areas can be used powerfully by God. Whatever gift or talent we have should be used to the glory of God. It is likely that Apollos, who was described as a "learned man, with a thorough knowledge of the Scriptures," having been a native of the Greek city of Alexandria (Acts 18:24-25), had such expertise in this area, which made Paul's weakness more obvious. Whatever the case, eloquent speaking does not seem to have been Paul's strength. This does not mean that Paul was not powerful and effective. His strengths were to be found in other areas, such as spiritual knowledge.

Don't Muzzle the Ox

> [7]Was it a sin for me to lower myself in order to elevate you by preaching the gospel of God to you free of charge? [8]I robbed other churches by receiving support from them so as to serve you. [9]And when I was with you and needed something, I was not a burden to anyone, for the brothers who came from Macedonia supplied what I needed. I have kept myself from being a burden to you in any way, and will continue to do so. [10]As surely as the truth of Christ is in me, nobody in the regions of Achaia will stop this boasting of mine.

In 1 Corinthians 9, Paul deals with the Corinthians' critical attitudes toward him and their hesitancy and unwillingness to financially meet his needs. Although he argues persuasively that he had the right to receive his living from the gospel, he decided to exercise his freedom and not take their support:

> But I have not used any of these rights. And I am not writing this in the hope that you will do such things for me. I would rather die than have anyone deprive me of this boast (1 Corinthians 9:15).

Paul's strategy was to convict the Corinthians of their terrible and striking ingratitude for all that he had done for them by refusing their support.

Paul is asking if it was wrong for him to humble himself and preach the gospel to them free of charge (11:7). Again, Paul is being facetious, but he is using it in a powerful way. The Corinthians accused him of *robbing* them when he had formerly expected *support* from them. Their hypocrisy was that they did not seem to mind when other churches supported him while he was in Corinth, but when he expected the Corinthians to support him, it was considered robbery!

What is important to see in Paul's heart is the extent to which he was willing to sacrifice in order for the Corinthians to do well spiritually. The temptation would be to move into an authoritative mode and command the Corinthians to repent and offer him the support to which he was entitled. However, in this situation, Paul felt the need to forego his rights as an apostle and give the Corinthians no further room for criticism—in the hopes that he would move them to repentance by his example.

Toppling the Superheroes

> *[11]Why? Because I do not love you? God knows I do! [12]And I will keep on doing what I am doing in order to cut the ground from under those who want an opportunity to be considered equal with us in the things they boast about.*

Paul taught in 1 Corinthians 13:7-8 that love never fails and that "it always protects, always trusts, always hopes, always perseveres." Someone with impure motives could never sustain the level of sacrifice to which Paul had committed himself. He had decided to do whatever was necessary, and for however long it was necessary, to prove to the Corinthians the depth of his love for them. His intention, in no uncertain terms, was to undermine the influence of the false teachers and to expose their empty boasts about being equal with the other apostles.

Removing the Masks

> *[13]For such men are false apostles, deceitful workmen, masquerading as apostles of Christ. [14]And no wonder, for*

Satan himself masquerades as an angel of light. [15]It is not
surprising, then, if his servants masquerade as servants of
righteousness. Their end will be what their actions deserve.

This is, by far, the strongest indictment of those who
were pulling the Corinthians away from Paul. He cuts them
no slack, shows absolutely no mercy and has no intention of taking any prisoners. Up to this point, Paul has
shown a great deal of sensitivity in dealing with the deli-
cate nature of the problems in Corinth. Paul is now focused on one thing—to completely expose the false teachers, thus showing the Corinthians exactly who has been
influencing and leading them. It seems logical that Paul
waited until the end of his letter to use such strong language so that he could build his argument in the most
convincing and credible way. Without the foundation of
first explaining to them the reasons for his decisions and
changes in plans, exposing the false teachers might have
caused the Corinthians to react negatively to him.

To Paul, the whole thing was a masquerade. These
people were exactly opposite of what they claimed to be.
They claimed to be apostles, but only qualified as false
apostles. They were obviously working, but were doing
so deceitfully. The Corinthians were being seriously deceived by this masquerade, but Paul points out that the
one responsible for it all is Satan, who always masquerades as an angel of light. It is not surprising that these
false teachers, who Paul refers to as Satan's servants,
would appear righteous. When your spiritual eyes are bad,
you are easily fooled.

The Wise and the Foolish

[16]I repeat: Let no one take me for a fool. But if you do,
then receive me just as you would a fool, so that I may do
a little boasting. [17]In this self-confident boasting I am not
talking as the Lord would, but as a fool. [18]Since many are
boasting in the way the world does, I too will boast. [19]You

gladly put up with fools since you are so wise! [20]*In fact, you even put up with anyone who enslaves you or exploits you or takes advantage of you or pushes himself forward or slaps you in the face.* [21]*To my shame I admit that we were too weak for that!*

Paul continues using strong language to describe the false teachers. However, now he turns to the Corinthians themselves in a much stronger way, using a play on words to argue his credibility. Paul wants it understood that he is no fool. However, if the Corinthians had gotten to the point where they were considering Paul a fool, then they would certainly have no problem with his foolish arguments. He admits that he was not arguing as the Lord, but since that was no longer the standard of the Corinthians anyway— in that they were allowing themselves to be influenced by the foolish arguments of the false teachers—they would have no reason to hold that against him.

The false teachers had been advocating that it was Paul who was exploiting the Corinthians—which is probably the reason for Paul's discussion in 1 Corinthians 9 about his right to be supported, but his refusal to exert that right. Paul is turning the charges of exploitation on the false teachers and rebuking the Corinthians for allowing themselves to be so manipulated.

A Life to Back It Up

[21b]*What anyone else dares to boast about—I am speaking as a fool—I also dare to boast about.* [22]*Are they Hebrews? So am I. Are they Israelites? So am I. Are they Abraham's descendants? So am I.* [23]*Are they servants of Christ? (I am out of my mind to talk like this.) I am more. I have worked much harder, been in prison more frequently, been flogged more severely, and been exposed to death again and again.* [24]*Five times I received from the Jews the forty lashes minus one.* [25]*Three times I was beaten with rods, once I was stoned, three times I was shipwrecked, I spent a night and a day in the open sea,* [26]*I have been constantly on the move. I have been in danger from rivers, in danger from*

*bandits, in danger from my own countrymen, in danger from
Gentiles; in danger in the city, in danger in the country, in
danger at sea; and in danger from false brothers. [27]I have
labored and toiled and have often gone without sleep; I have
known hunger and thirst and have often gone without food;
I have been cold and naked. [28]Besides everything else, I face
daily the pressure of my concern for all the churches. [29]Who
is weak, and I do not feel weak? Who is led into sin, and I do
not inwardly burn?*

In the world an impressive résumé can open many
doors to a successful career, and it is a basic requirement
in order to evaluate the qualifications of someone being
considered for employment. From what Paul writes here
(11:21b-29), it seems that the false teachers in Corinth
were flashing their résumés around the fellowship, im-
pressing and winning over the Corinthians. Paul now clues
us in to the background of these men. They were obviously taking great pride in being Jewish and were probably using their knowledge of the Old Testament in a
manipulative sort of way to impress the Greek (Gentile)
brothers and sisters. Paul states emphatically that he also
was a Hebrew, an Israelite and a descendant of Abraham.

The Jews took great pride in their nation and were
known in the ancient world, as they are today, for their
nationalistic fervor. Jesus, ushering in the new covenant,
brought a universal teaching that could no longer be contained within the borders of only one nation. Therefore,
the value of Judaism as a way of life, as well as the need
of Israel as a nation, was quickly coming to an end. Jesus
taught, "Do not think that I have come to abolish the Law
or the Prophets; I have not come to abolish them but to
fulfill them" (Matthew 5:17). The purpose for Judaism was
to lay the foundation for Christianity. It never pointed to
itself as the be-all, end-all, but always pointed to what
was destined to fulfill it. Due to the nature of the two covenants, that one was to fulfill the other, anyone wanting

to hold on to the old obviously would have a problem accepting the new. We see this tension in the relationship between Jesus and the Jews constantly.

One clash of the old and the new is recorded in John 8, when Jesus is teaching on the universality of sin and the new way for this sin to be atoned. After Jesus taught on the need to be set free, the Jews defensively appealed to the fact that they were Abraham's descendants and had never been slaves to anyone (John 8:33). Jesus replied by saying,

> *"I tell you the truth, everyone who sins is a slave to sin. Now a slave has no permanent place in the family, but a son belongs to it forever. So if the Son sets you free, you will be free indeed" (John 8:34-36).*

From this time on, being a Jew no longer has anything to do with being forgiven of sins. Therefore, it is no longer relevant to the spiritual life or one's relationship with God. Any appeal to being a Jew is now an appeal to the flesh, in contrast to the spirit. And yet, often Paul's opposition would use their Jewish background as part of their tactic to undermine his credibility. This is clear here in 2 Corinthians 11, as well as in other verses in the New Testament such as Philippians 3:4b-6:

> *If anyone else thinks he has reasons to put confidence in the flesh, I have more: circumcised on the eighth day, of the people of Israel, of the tribe of Benjamin, a Hebrew of Hebrews; in regard to the law, a Pharisee; as for zeal, persecuting the church; as for legalistic righteousness, faultless.*

The issue that the false teachers had to deal with was the impressiveness of Paul, both in his Jewish background and also in how God was using him as a Christian. Even though Paul was conscience-stricken when referring to his accomplishments (which is why he says in 11:23, "I

am out of my mind to talk like this"), he was also aware
of its power in persuading the worldly minded. Even from
a worldly point of view, the résumé of the false teachers
was no match for Paul's world-renowned accomplishments in Judaism.

Beyond his qualifications in Judaism were the real
qualifications of Paul's spiritual life in Christ. The suffering and hardship that Paul had experienced were the fulfillment of God's words to Ananias:

> *This man is my chosen instrument to carry my name before*
> *the Gentiles and their kings and before the people of Israel.*
> *I will show him how much he must suffer for my name (Acts*
> *9:15-16).*

His sufferings were not only indicative of the truth of God's
word, but were also indicative of the fact that Paul had,
indeed, been chosen by God for a special mission.

Some of these experiences can be found in the book
of Acts. To mention a few, Paul was flogged in Philippi
(Acts 16:23), stoned in Lystra (Acts 14:19), shipwrecked
on the island of Malta (Acts 27:1-44), and in danger from
fellow Jews from Antioch and Iconium (Acts 14:19). Not
only was Paul called to live a physically demanding life,
he also carried the emotional pressure and responsibility
for the well-being of all the churches he had planted.

Paul's list of intense experiences and sufferings shows
him to be a true servant of Christ, and also shows why
the theme of weakness turning into strength is such an
important part of his argument throughout the letter. Because of the legalistic, critical nature of the Corinthians,
it was very easy for them to focus on the weaknesses in
Paul's life. Yet, what they had failed to realize was that
the suffering and intense trials, which in some ways vali-
dated Paul as an apostle and servant of Christ, also revealed his humanity and weaknesses. Paradoxically, our

weaknesses always come to the surface during our trials, but then God works to transform our weaknesses into strengths.

A New Approach to Boasting

>   *[30]If I must boast, I will boast of the things that show my weakness. [31]The God and Father of the Lord Jesus, who is to be praised forever, knows that I am not lying. [32]In Damascus the governor under King Aretas had the city of the Damascenes guarded in order to arrest me. [33]But I was lowered in a basket from a window in the wall and slipped through his hands.*

Boasting of the things that showed their weakness was a critical point Paul needed the Corinthians to understand. In light of the transforming power of our spiritual trials, weakness now becomes something of which we boast and can no longer be used against us in a critical, undermining way.

Paul's mention of being lowered in a basket to escape the persecution in Damascus may be simply a parenthetical statement after the introduction of the more prominent theme that will continue into chapter 12. However, it would seem, in keeping with the context, that Paul sees it as a powerful symbol and reminder of how God works. Shortly after becoming a disciple, the once bold and zealous persecutor of the church did not vigorously march out of the city under his own power, but he was huddled in a basket, dependent on the help and goodwill of those he had once persecuted for his freedom. For the once proud Saul of Tarsus it was an enlightening introduction to a new spiritual life similar to that of his new Lord, who was born to peasant parents, rejected in his home town and crucified on a cross. It was the beginning of a whole new way of thinking about how God gets things done!

That Paul was willing to bring up such an event at this point in his letter shows just how differently he thought than those proud false teachers. The good news is that in Jesus Christ we do not any longer have to hide our weaknesses, but we can bring them to him and into the light where God works through them for his purposes. Paul clearly understood this.

10
Perfected by Weakness

2 Corinthians 12:1-10

In this section Paul is probably more transparent about his inner life and experiences than at any point in his letters. He openly shares with the Corinthians one of the most personally inspirational and revealing moments of his life. He, however, does none of this to draw attention to himself. It is God's power perfected in our weaknesses that he wants to highlight. This becomes clear as we look carefully at this section of the letter.

Into the Third Heaven

> *12:1I must go on boasting. Although there is nothing to be gained, I will go on to visions and revelations from the Lord. 2I know a man in Christ who fourteen years ago was caught up to the third heaven. Whether it was in the body or out of the body I do not know—God knows. 3And I know that this man—whether in the body or apart from the body I do not know, but God knows— 4was caught up to paradise. He heard inexpressible things, things that man is not permitted to tell.*

This passage probably raises the most questions about 2 Corinthians than any other part of the letter. What does Paul mean by "visions and revelations"? Who was the man Paul is referring to? Where is the third heaven? What does "in or out of the body" mean? These are all important and logical questions to ask.

Paul is continuing the theme of boasting in weaknesses and includes as part of that boasting an experience that took place fourteen years earlier when he received revelations from the Lord. Paul has become somewhat apologetic in his boasting, knowing that must deal carefully with the feelings that the Corinthians have toward him and toward the false teachers. It was important for the Corinthians to understand that God was revealing things to Paul in a unique way because of his mission to take the gospel to the Gentiles. Yet, visions and revelations, as they are today in the religious world, can be very subjective in nature and easily falsified. The last thing that Paul wanted was to start a boasting match about revelations, especially in light of the confusion already present over the spiritual gifts in Corinth (1 Corinthians 12-14).

Perhaps Paul refers to himself in the third person (12:1-4) in order to take the focus off himself and to prevent his opponents from accusing him of self-commendation. (That Paul is referring to himself is clear from 12:7 where he writes, "To keep me from becoming conceited because of these surpassingly great revelations....") It is almost impossible to pinpoint exactly when these revelations took place, even though Paul mentions that they happened fourteen years earlier than the writing of 2 Corinthians.

Throughout Paul's ministry, he received visions and revelations from the Lord to guide him and to provide him the truth that needed to be preached. For example, Acts 22:17-18 states that while praying in the Jerusalem temple after his conversion, Paul fell into a trance and saw the Lord telling him to leave the city. In Galatians 2:2, Paul mentions that the reason he returned to Jerusalem was in "response to a revelation." Acts 16:9 records that Paul had a vision in which he saw a man from Macedonia begging for him to come and help him.

From the evidence of the New Testament it appears that these experiences happened periodically throughout Paul's ministry. However, the experience mentioned here in 2 Corinthians 12 appears to be completely different from all of the other revelations and visions he had received from the Lord. Paul writes that he heard "inexpressible things, things that man is not permitted to tell" (12:4). Normally, Paul is quick to relate the contents of special revelations. However, for some reason, this one was not to be communicated.

Paul's reference to the "third heaven" indicates that the thinking in his time reflected a *layered* conception of the spiritual world. In our world, we speak in terms of a vertical spiritual realm with heaven being "up" and hell being "down." It is very difficult to determine exactly what the reference to the third heaven means. There is no other mention of it in the Bible, nor do we find it mentioned in other writings of the time. We do have references to five, seven and ten heavens in the literature of the early rabbis and in the pseudepigraphon or apocrypha, which indicates that the idea of heavens varied in the ancient world. Exactly what the different layers represent is still unknown to us, but it seems likely, due to the type of revelation Paul received, that the third heaven was the highest level. What the first and second layers contained can only be conjectured.

The phrase "whether it was in the body or out of the body I do not know—God knows" (12:2), was also a different experience than what Paul was used to. Visions and revelations were normally "in body." In other words, Paul would see a vision, have a dream or fall into a trance. In this situation, Paul wrote that he "was caught up to paradise" (12:4) and did not know whether he left his body or stayed in his body to receive the vision. Whatever occurred was not the focus of what Paul was writing, but rather that he had heard the deep mysteries of existence that not only cannot be verbally expressed, but carry with them a secrecy forbidding their communication.

No Bragging Rights

> [5]I will boast about a man like that, but I will not boast about
> myself, except about my weaknesses. [6]Even if I should choose
> to boast, I would not be a fool, because I would be speaking
> the truth. But I refrain, so no one will think more of me than
> is warranted by what I do or say.

Paul is definitely using wordplay in order to make his point. The fact that he had received a totally unique revelation, in contrast to the revelation that was available to the church in general (1 Corinthians 12:4-11), needed to be fully understood by the Corinthians. The receiving of that revelation confirmed Paul's position and authority as an apostle sent from God. Paul had every right to boast about that experience and to use it to confirm his mission.

However, at the same time, Paul fully realized that he was not worthy of such a position or of such a revelation. That is why he says, "but I will not boast about myself" (12:5). Paul had been chosen and did not even deserve to be called an apostle. He mentally disciplined himself to remain cognizant of this fact.

> I thank Christ Jesus our Lord, who has given me strength,
> that he considered me faithful, appointing me to his service.
> Even though I was once a blasphemer and a persecutor and
> a violent man, I was shown mercy because I acted in igno-
> rance and unbelief. The grace of our Lord was poured out
> on me abundantly, along with the faith and love that are in
> Christ Jesus (1 Timothy 1:12-14).

> For I am the least of the apostles and do not even de-
> serve to be called an apostle, because I persecuted the church
> of God. But by the grace of God I am what I am, and his
> grace to me was not without effect. No, I worked harder than
> all of them—yet not I, but the grace of God that was with me
> (1 Corinthians 15:9-10).

In one sense Paul had every right to boast, but in an-other sense it would produce more problems than it would solve. The issue of weakness is again interjected as Paul continues to develop the idea and moves toward his most powerful point. There is nothing wrong about boasting in our weaknesses because of the humility that accompanies such boasting. Pride is extremely offended by any discussion of weakness and can never truly boast in it. The prideful person has no alternative but to deal with his weaknesses, at least to some degree due to the obviousness of his human nature, but to boast in them is impossible for him. We should not overlook how differently Paul approaches all of this.

Never Promised a Rose Garden

> *[7]To keep me from becoming conceited because of these surpassingly great revelations, there was given me a thorn in my flesh, a messenger of Satan, to torment me. [8]Three times I pleaded with the Lord to take it away from me.*

Boasting in weakness is never easily done. It takes deep spiritual convictions and a deep trust in God. Paul's ability to boast in his weakness came only after intense encounters with both God and himself. He had to be put into a position where he had no choice but to see his weakness—with no possibility of escaping through the deception that pride so easily offers. "Surpassingly great revelations" (12:7), though extremely informative, are never good for our pride, and so it was with Paul. His thorn in the flesh was at least one way God chose to offset the power of arrogance and conceit.

There has been much debate over what exactly the thorn in the flesh was. The idiom, "thorn in the flesh," in and of itself offers no real clues as to what Paul was suffering from. The phrase "in the flesh" points us toward thinking of it as a physical ailment or hardship. However, it could be in reference to the whole of Paul's life in the physical realm. There are a multitude of possibilities historically suggested: epilepsy, malaria, some type of eye disease, lust and persecution.

The only truth we know about this thorn is that we cannot know for sure what it was! Biblical conjecture takes up much of the time of many biblical scholars, but its labor always ends up in the same place—the unknown. We must always remember that a theory is just that, a theory. The enduring ability of many theories never brings them closer to the truth. Some would have us believe that the longer a theory exists, the more probability it has of being right. However, the fact that a theory remains a theory for a long period of time indicates the lack of evidence either to prove or disprove it.

Whatever his thorn in the flesh was, Paul considered it sent from Satan to torment him. Though Satan attacks us for our destruction, God is able to use those attacks for our spiritual good. This calls to mind Job's situation in the Old Testament. After negotiating with the Lord, Satan believed that Job would crack under the pressure of human suffering. Suffering is definitely one of Satan's main weapons to discourage us and cause us to lose our faith. Begging the Lord to remove the thorn shows the intense pressure Paul felt and also his lack of insight at this point into the value of suffering for our spiritual growth. God was not *withholding* his blessings at this point, but was pointing to the direction where the blessings could be found.

From Dread to Delight

> [9]*But he said to me, "My grace is sufficient for you, for my power is made perfect in weakness." Therefore I will boast all the more gladly about my weaknesses, so that Christ's power may rest on me.* [10]*That is why, for Christ's sake, I delight in weaknesses, in insults, in hardships, in persecutions, in difficulties. For when I am weak, then I am strong.*

At times of intense suffering or hardship, the answer, "My grace is sufficient for you, for my power is made perfect in weakness," seems a bit abstract, failing to meet the practical need of alleviating the suffering. It is easy to believe that the main remedy for suffering is the removal of it. At least, that is what our flesh cries out for! Our world is full of painkillers and other medications whose purpose is to remove suffering. Frequently alcohol and drug addiction are the result of an attempt to alleviate something in life that is causing great anxiety and pain. Many hospitals now promise that they can make surgical operations pain-free in order attract more business. A deeper understanding of grace is not exactly part of their advertising campaign!

Removing suffering entirely from our lives, though pleasing to the flesh, causes great damage to our spiritual lives. An environment devoid of suffering affords fewer opportunities for God to demonstrate his power and no opportunity for us to learn to trust in that power. The same is true about our weaknesses. Often we hear of turning our weaknesses into strengths, which admittedly is a much-needed transformation in all of our lives. However, that is not really what Paul has in mind in this context. If all the weakness in our lives is transformed into strength, then where is the opportunity for God's power to be seen? Paul has in mind another transformation, and it does not involve the removal of our weaknesses, but the transformation of our *perspective* on our weaknesses.

Sometimes we have the idea that one day all of our weaknesses will be gone and we will be strong disciples. The longer I live, the more apparent it becomes that our weaknesses remain with us the rest of our lives. What changes is not the basic weakness but our ability to accomplish the purposes of God despite our human limitations. The power of God comes in when we are able, for example, to love when our weakness is that we are unloving, to be sensitive when our weakness is insensitivity, to be patient when our weakness is a quick temper, to be bold when our weakness is being cowardly. The weakness is necessary for the power of God to be seen.

Notice that Paul does not write, "Therefore, I will boast all the more gladly *that my weaknesses are gone,* so that Christ's power may rest on me." Rather he writes, "Therefore, I will boast all the more gladly *about my weaknesses,* so that Christ's power may rest on me" (12:9, emphasis added). Paul was able to look at his weakness and see God. In the context of Paul's relationship with the critical Corinthians, it was his hope that when they saw Paul's weaknesses in the context of all that he had accomplished for God, which included the planting of the church in Corinth, they would see the power of God.

We can see the transformation of Paul's perspective about life when he writes, "I *delight* in weaknesses..." (12:10, emphasis added). He had been transformed from a begging apostle, disgruntled about his situation, to an apostle who delighted in what he once begged God to remove from him. Paul had indeed been blessed! To reach the capability of experiencing this level of intense suffering (12:10) still being able to say, "I delight" in the experience, is a statement of the ultimate victory. While facing our weaknesses and failures is usually thought to be negative, it is really an experience that can make us much more aware and appreciative of the power and strength of God. Accepting our weaknesses is a vital part of achieving the state of *delight* that Paul was able to experience. There is no doubt that God worked powerfully in the life of the apostle Paul. Suffering was a crucial part of that working. Failing to embrace this suffering robs God of the opportunity to work as gloriously in our lives.

11
Prepare for Paul's Coming

2 Corinthians 12:11-13:4

In this section of the letter it again becomes obvious how uneasy Paul was with listing his personal accomplishments and how God was presently using him to argue his case before the Corinthians. Though boasting was a part of his past life, as a disciple, he gave God all of the credit and glory. However, if boasting could somehow help the Corinthians to come to their senses and disarm the boasting of the false teachers, Paul was willing to engage them on the battleground they had themselves chosen.

Apostle with a Capital "A"

12:11I have made a fool of myself, but you drove me to it. I ought to have been commended by you, for I am not in the least inferior to the "super-apostles," even though I am nothing. 12The things that mark an apostle—signs, wonders and miracles—were done among you with great perseverance. 13How were you inferior to the other churches, except that I was never a burden to you? Forgive me this wrong!

Paul was in no way going to give the false teachers home-court advantage. If the Corinthians criticized Paul for commending himself, as they probably did, they needed to realize their own responsibility for allowing the spread of pride in their church—particularly by allowing themselves to be persuaded by the same self-commendating methods of the false teachers. Paul should never have been made to feel that it was necessary to flaunt his spiritual accomplishments. We need to keep in mind that throughout this letter, Paul avoids speaking directly to the false teachers, as if not to grant them any recognition at all. However, he, at the same time, fully realizes that they will be reading his letter with careful scrutiny.

Paul has spent a great deal of energy in 2 Corinthians showing that weakness in the flesh is not necessarily an indication of weakness in the spirit. Although there were weaknesses in Paul's life, he still refused to be considered inferior to the so-called "super-apostles" in Corinth. And what had been so blatantly overlooked were the miracles God had worked in Paul's life, proving that he was a true apostle.

The original twelve apostles were uniquely endowed with the ability to perform miracles, and more importantly, were the only ones who could pass the ability on to others. See Acts 8:14-18, quoted here in part:

> *When the apostles in Jerusalem heard that Samaria had accepted the word of God, they sent Peter and John to them. When they arrived, they prayed for them that they might receive the Holy Spirit, because the Holy Spirit had not yet come upon any of them; they had simply been baptized into the name of the Lord Jesus. Then Peter and John placed their hands on them, and they received the Holy Spirit.*
>
> *When Simon saw that the Spirit was given at the laying on of the apostles' hands, he offered them money and said, "Give me also this ability so that everyone on whom I lay my hands may receive the Holy Spirit."*

The context of this passage involves Philip the evangelist who had gone to the city of Samaria and "proclaimed the Christ there" (Acts 8:5). The passage goes on, "When the crowds heard Philip and saw the miraculous signs he did, they all paid close attention to what he said" (Acts 8:6). Philip was a powerful preacher, able to perform impressive miracles. And yet, he was not able to give the Samaritans the Holy Spirit. He was only able to baptize them in the name of the Lord Jesus.

In order to understand the reference to the Holy Spirit here in Acts 8, we must understand an important distinction the Bible makes. On the Day of Pentecost, as recorded in Acts 2:38, Peter said, "Repent and be baptized, every one of you, in the name of Jesus Christ for the forgiveness of your sins. And you will receive the gift of the Holy Spirit." It is clear from this scripture that everyone who believes, repents of their sins and is baptized receives the gift of the Holy Spirit. This is often referred to as "the indwelling of the Holy Spirit." This is the meaning of 2 Corinthians 1:21-22:

> *Now it is God who makes both us and you stand firm in Christ. He anointed us, set his seal of ownership on us, and put his Spirit in our hearts as a deposit, guaranteeing what is to come.*

And yet, Acts 8:16 says, "the Holy Spirit had not yet come upon any of them." The apparent discrepancy is a result of the different ways that "Holy Spirit" is being used. "The gifts of the Holy Spirit" are an entirely different entity from the indwelling of the Spirit. Paul points this out in 1 Corinthians 12:4-11:

> *There are different kinds of gifts, but the same Spirit. There are different kinds of service, but the same Lord. There are different kinds of working, but the same God works all of them in all men.*
> *Now to each one the manifestation of the Spirit is given for the common good. To one there is given through the Spirit the message of wisdom, to another the message of knowledge by means of the same Spirit, to another faith by the same Spirit, to another gifts of healing by that one Spirit, to another miraculous powers, to another prophecy, to another distinguishing between spirits, to another speaking in different kinds of tongues, and to still another the interpretation of tongues. All these are the work of one and the same Spirit, and he gives them to each one, just as he determines.*

Though everybody had the same Spirit, not everybody had the same gift. In fact, not everyone even had a gift. It is these gifts of the Spirit that the Samaritans had not received, which were important to their having the word of God and which were the reason Peter and John went to Samaria. Notice the wording again: "the Spirit was given at the laying on of the apostles' hands" (Acts 8:18). It was only the *apostles* who had the authority to give the ability to perform the miraculous.

Though Paul was not one of the original Twelve, he was an apostle, and the Corinthians were well aware of his qualifications. He was the one who had brought the gifts of the Holy Spirit to Corinth in the first place! It was through the laying on of his hands that the Corinthians were able to possess the gifts mentioned in 1 Corinthians 12. Paul not only gave them this ability, but with the use of these gifts himself, he ministered to the Corinthians "with great perseverance" (12:12).

Paul's facetious question, "How were you inferior to the other churches, except that I was never a burden to you?" (12:13) makes a penetrating point. The church in Corinth was every bit as great a congregation as any other church of its time. It was in no way inferior to any other church. The one difference was that Paul was not "a burden" to them, which probably means that he was not receiving support from them as the other apostles were receiving from their churches. (The reference in the next verse (12:14) of Paul not wanting their possessions supports this interpretation, as well as does 1 Corinthians 9:1-5.)

Fatherly Concern

> [14]Now I am ready to visit you for the third time, and I will not be a burden to you, because what I want is not your possessions but you. After all, children should not have to save up for their parents, but parents for their children. [15]So

*I will very gladly spend for you everything I have and ex-
pend myself as well. If I love you more, will you love me
less? [16]Be that as it may, I have not been a burden to you.
Yet, crafty fellow that I am, I caught you by trickery! [17]Did I
exploit you through any of the men I sent you? [18]I urged
Titus to go to you and I sent our brother with him. Titus did
not exploit you, did he? Did we not act in the same spirit
and follow the same course?*

It is somewhat amazing, and definitely tragic, how
often the issue of Paul's support comes up in this letter.
This passage makes it clear what the real issue was behind the Corinthians' lack of support for Paul. He must
have been deeply hurt that the Corinthians had allowed
themselves to be convinced that Paul was after their
money and possessions. This is clear from his use of
the parent-child illustration. All that Paul really wanted
was to have back the hearts of the Corinthians. That the
Corinthians felt tricked and exploited not only deeply
hurt Paul but was also a sobering testimony of how false
and divisive teaching destroys relationships and ultimately, the church. The evidence was clear. Not only
had Paul not manipulated the Corinthians, but neither
had Titus nor any of the other men whom Paul had sent
to them.

...And Justice for All

*[19]Have you been thinking all along that we have been
defending ourselves to you? We have been speaking in the
sight of God as those in Christ; and everything we do, dear
friends, is for your strengthening. [20]For I am afraid that when
I come I may not find you as I want you to be, and you may
not find me as you want me to be. I fear that there may be
quarreling, jealousy, outbursts of anger, factions, slander,
gossip, arrogance and disorder. [21]I am afraid that when I
come again my God will humble me before you, and I will
be grieved over many who have sinned earlier and have not
repented of the impurity, sexual sin and debauchery in which
they have indulged.*

The main fear of Paul (12:20) was that when he arrived in Corinth, he was going to find all kinds of problems. The severity of these problems, if not resolved by repentance by the time he arrived, would force Paul's hand to have to deal strongly with them. If that were the case, then the Corinthians will not find him as they would like him to be (12:20). Previously, in 1 Corinthians 4:18-21, Paul wrote:

> *Some of you have become arrogant, as if I were not coming to you. But I will come to you very soon, if the Lord is willing, and then I will find out not only how these arrogant people are talking, but what power they have. For the kingdom of God is not a matter of talk but of power. What do you prefer? Shall I come to you with a whip, or in love and with a gentle spirit?*

In other words, Paul coming to Corinth with a whip was not what the Corinthians would have desired. In fact, it was exactly the opposite of how they would want Paul to be. In the middle of being disciplined, it is hard to trust that those exercising the discipline are doing it for our own good.

The real problem in Corinth was sin. The quarreling, jealousy, anger, factions, slander, gossip, arrogance and disorder should have been the focus of the brothers and sisters in Corinth, not the weaknesses and what they perceived to be inconsistencies in Paul's life. One thing is clear, if the Corinthians were not going to deal with the problem, then Paul was. Paul was being generous when he wrote, "I fear that there may be quarreling..." and more (12:20). There was really no "maybe" in Corinth. The sin was there, and the only action that would have any effect on the situation would be genuine repentance.

It is amazing what repentance will do. It has the same effect as one's baptism. No disciple can ever forget the incredible feeling of coming up out of the waters of baptism and knowing that all of his sins have just been forgiven! The sad thing is that often many disciples fall back into some sin of the past and, even after repenting, do not feel forgiven. They instead carry a constant sense of dread or failure. But, it was never God's will for his children to experience the burden of not being able to spiritually resolve things in our relationship with him.

> *But if we walk in the light, as he is in the light, we have fellowship with one another, and the blood of Jesus, his Son, purifies us from all sin (1 John 1:7).*

"Walking in the light" is living a life of openness, humility and obedience. It simply means that if we live as disciples, then the blood of Jesus, which we first encountered in baptism, continually purifies our sins. The Greek verbs in this passage are not in past tense but in the present, and carry the idea of continuous action. In other words, the blood of Christ is *always* working as we walk in the light. The Corinthians were a only a step away from putting the past behind them and experiencing a new beginning in their relationship with God, as well as their relationship with Paul—not that this was going to be easy. Impurity, sexual sin and debauchery have a powerful and enslaving effect on us. Yet, the power of sin is no match for the power of God. We must always remember that, as disciples, repentance is always possible in every area of life.

12
Examine Yourselves

2 Corinthians 13

Although Paul has been extremely sensitive and tactful in considering the feelings and spiritual immaturity of the Corinthians, he wants it known in no uncertain terms that sin is going to be dealt with in Corinth. Because of the divisive and critical nature of the congregation, it would seem probable to assume that Paul was going to be flooded with all sorts of accusations and complaints that the disciples had against one another. In order to prepare for this onslaught Paul quotes from Deuteronomy 19:15, which sets forth how guilt was often established under the old law. This method would have worked quite well in Corinth, especially when trying to decipher who the guilty parties were, having been absent himself.

No Fear in Love

> *[13:1]This will be my third visit to you. "Every matter must be established by the testimony of two or three witnesses." [2]I already gave you a warning when I was with you the second time. I now repeat it while absent: On my return I will not spare those who sinned earlier or any of the others, [3]since you are demanding proof that Christ is speaking through me. He is not weak in dealing with you, but is powerful among you. [4]For to be sure, he was crucified in weakness, yet he lives by God's power. Likewise, we are weak in him, yet by God's power we will live with him to serve you.*

As we have already discussed in the commentary on the "letters of recommendation" in 3:1-3, the Corinthians were apparently demanding proof of Paul's authority or credentials as an apostle. The NIV translators render the

Greek word *zateo* as "demand" (13:3) which, according to the overall context of the letter, is probably the best translation. The Greek word literally means "to ask or to seek something." However, it is more than obvious that the Corinthians were well beyond a mere desire to verify whether Paul was a true apostle. Because of their criticalness, they had definitely reached the demanding stage. What they were not expecting was that they were about to get their fill of evidence—and probably a lot more than they would have ever imagined needing. The Corinthians were about to personally experience Paul's main point in this letter: God's power is perfectly demonstrated only through weakness. The Corinthians had seen only the weakness of Paul; now they were on the verge of seeing his power. The same principle can be seen in the physical life of Christ. The world saw Jesus as weak and defeated as he died in poverty on the cross. However, what appeared weak was simply setting the stage to demonstrate God's ultimate power over death, the resurrection.

And yet, all of this resurrection power had a very practical side. It seems from the context that Paul is going to be confronting the sin in the church, which will demonstrate the power of God in Paul's life.

Truth Will Prevail

> [5]Examine yourselves to see whether you are in the faith; test yourselves. Do you not realize that Christ Jesus is in you—unless, of course, you fail the test? [6]And I trust that you will discover that we have not failed the test. [7]Now we pray to God that you will not do anything wrong. Not that people will see that we have stood the test but that you will do what is right even though we may seem to have failed. [8]For we cannot do anything against the truth, but only for the truth. [9]We are glad whenever we are weak but you are strong; and our prayer is for your perfection. [10]This is why I write these things when I am absent, that when I come I may not have to be harsh in my use of authority—the authority the Lord gave me for building you up, not for tearing you down.

This passage gives us some important insight into the biblical definition of faith. One of the most widespread and erroneous assumptions in the religious world today is that faith is an experience that has no objective definition. It is purely subjective, and therefore, individually defined. Denominationalism has fallen into the trap of liberal theology and philosophy, which has put man at the center of the universe rather than God. Though God is mentioned in most churches, truth and faith are no longer defined from God's point of view but from man's.

This false understanding of faith puts all "Christian" relationships in the mode of acceptance and tolerance and prohibits any real examination and questioning of one another's faith. In essence, no biblical discipling of one another is possible with this definition. Instead of "speaking the truth in love," as the Bible commands, in order to "grow up into him who is the Head, that is, Christ" (Ephesians 4:15), we are forced to accept whatever someone else accepts as truth.

Though faith is a personal experience, its ultimate definition is not personal. The Bible teaches that there is one faith (Ephesians 4:5). That means our personal experience must embrace this one faith. Practically speaking, it makes a difference *what* we believe—an eternal difference!

The challenge from Paul is for the Corinthians to examine their faith, to test it to see if they were even still in the faith. In other words, an examination of this type assumes the possibility that they might have no longer been in the faith. Some, in order to defend the "once saved, always saved" doctrine, might want to argue that the Corinthians never really had any faith at all. So to them, the issue is not whether or not the Corinthians lost their salvation, but rather that the Corinthians never had any real faith to begin with. However, that is not exactly how

Paul describes the Corinthians in 1 Corinthians 1:1-8 when he writes:

> *To the church of God in Corinth, to those sanctified in Christ Jesus and called to be holy, together with all those everywhere who call on the name of our Lord Jesus Christ— their Lord and ours...*
>
> *I always thank God for you because of his grace given you in Christ Jesus. For in him you have been enriched in every way—in all your speaking and in all your knowledge —because our testimony about Christ was confirmed in you. ...He will keep you strong to the end, so that you will be blameless on the day of our Lord Jesus Christ.*

This is not exactly a description of people with no saving faith! The important point here is that unless they repented, the Corinthians could lose the standing in Christ that they had.

Paul's appeal here is to the truth: "For we cannot do anything against the truth, but only for the truth" (13:8). Paul firmly believed that the Corinthians, in the end, would see the truth. Even in the midst of Paul's weakness, failure and inconsistency, as well as the deceitful scheming of the false teachers in Corinth, the truth was the only thing that would prevail. It's amazing, in the heat of controversy, how the truth can be as illusive as it apparently was in Corinth. Even though all of those involved in the controversy in Corinth have been gone for centuries, the truth about the situation lives on eternally and will be made even clearer on the day of judgment. Truth always triumphs in the end!

Paul closes out the body of his letter by stating that his goal for the Corinthians was always perfection (13:9). That is the goal of every father for his children. Not perfection in terms of being without sin—that goal is impossible for anybody to reach—but a spiritual maturity which guides and protects throughout life. This was the purpose of the authority that the Lord had given Paul as an apostle, for building up the Corinthians and not for tearing them down (13:10). Jesus had made it clear how authority was to be used in his kingdom when he said:

> *"You know that the rulers of the Gentiles lord it over them, and their high officials exercise authority over them. Not so with you. Instead, whoever wants to become great among you must be your servant, and whoever wants to be first must be your slave—just as the Son of Man did not come to be served, but to serve, and to give his life as a ransom for many" (Matthew 20:25-28).*

Jesus also said, "But I, when I am lifted up from the earth, will draw all men to myself" (John 12:32). Though unrecognized by the world, humility is always more powerful than arrogance and pride. It has a drawing effect on others, whereas pride and arrogance repel and keep people at a distance. Paul had made it clear throughout his correspondence with the Corinthians that this was his conviction. Through all of the criticism and lack of support, Paul held on to these eternal truths.

Whatever ended up happening between Paul and the Corinthians has been lost to the ravages of time. What time can never do is quench the effects of walking humbly as a disciple. Paul said that when he entered Corinth for the first time, he did so "in weakness and fear, and with much trembling" (1 Corinthians 2:3). Never succumbing to the temptation of easing his fear with pride and power, Paul trusted the power of God to shine through the dark clouds of his humanity. It was Paul's prayer that the Corinthians, by embracing the same humility, would somehow be able to see the power of God.

Final Farewells

> *[11]Finally, brothers, good-by. Aim for perfection, listen to my appeal, be of one mind, live in peace. And the God of*

love and peace will be with you.
    *[12]Greet one another with a holy kiss. [13]All the saints send
their greetings.*
    *[14]May the grace of the Lord Jesus Christ, and the love of
God, and the fellowship of the Holy Spirit be with you all.*

Paul brings his life-changing letter to a close with a few imperatives and some comforting thoughts. The quest for perfection, unity and peace always ensures the presence of God in our lives, fulfilling Jesus' promise,

> *"Ask and it will be given to you; seek and you will find; knock and the door will be opened to you. For everyone who asks receives; he who seeks finds; and to him who knocks, the door will be opened" (Matthew 7:7-8).*

God always stands ready to bring resolution and forgiveness to us, and simply asks that we first begin the search in our own hearts. The answers for the Corinthians' problems were there. The real question historically is, *Did the Corinthians heed Paul's advice and continue to experience the presence of God, the grace of the Lord Jesus Christ and the fellowship of the Holy Spirit? Or did they fail the test?* We have no choice but to wait until heaven to find out. The choice *we* have is to imitate the heart, teaching and ministry of Paul, as revealed in this letter, to be sure that we ourselves do not fail the test!

Epilogue

Throughout my Christian life, the letter of 2 Corinthians has been a very important letter to me. To list all of the reasons would probably involve the writing of another book, yet to mention a few hopefully will help you, the reader, to apply the message to your life as well.

Paul's perspective on life is one of the greatest treasures of this letter. Though the lessons God taught him were tough to learn, in that they came through intense circumstances, the result was a life truly dependent on God and a humility carved out of learning to accept the call of God regardless of where it led. Paul was a man full of gratitude, which is probably the greatest spiritual possession we can acquire. A person who learns gratitude, even in trying times, is a person free from the misery of bitterness, jealously, loneliness and self-pity.

How Paul viewed his ministry is what got him through the painful circumstances of bringing a young church to spiritual maturity. His ministry was his treasure and therefore was his shield against the criticalness of those he loved so dearly. His love for the people was the reason he was able to put all of his heart into it. The battle against the false teachers in Corinth was waged not because of malice or impure motives, but because his relationship with his brothers and sisters was his most valued possession. He was willing to do whatever was necessary to win back their love and loyalty. The news from Titus that the Corinthians were repenting was greater for Paul than all the gold and silver in the world.

What has also kept me coming back to the message of 2 Corinthians is the point Paul makes about the power of weakness from God's point of view. Weakness and power are partners only in the kingdom of God and testify that our God is, indeed, alive. This understanding of weakness is probably the most difficult spiritual principle to master in the kingdom of God. Yet, the understanding of it provides the key to attaining contentment, trust, humility and God-reliance. As long as the attainment of these spiritual attributes is the goal of our lives, we are destined to find ourselves, time and time again, returning to the pages of 2 Corinthians, studying diligently every sentence and every word with gratitude for having the opportunity of imitating the apostle Paul, one of God's most devoted disciples.

Notes

Chapter One

1. David A. Hubbard and Glenn W. Barker, eds., *Word Biblical Commentary* (Waco, Texas: Word Books, 1986), vol. 40, *2 Corinthians*, by Ralph P. Martin, 27-28; F.F. Bruce, ed., *The New International Commentary on the New Testament* (Grand Rapids, Michigan: Eerdmans Publishing Co., 1962), *Paul's Second Epistle to the Corinthians,* Philip E. Hughes, 38-40.
2. W. Bauer, F.W. Gingrich, and F.W. Danker, *A Greek-English Lexicon of the New Testament and Other Early Christian Literature* (2nd ed.; Chicago, Ill./London: University of Chicago, 1979), 109.

Chapter Seven

1. F.F. Bruce, ed., *The New International Commentary on the New Testament* (Grand Rapids, Michigan: Eerdmans Publishing Co., 1962), *Paul's Second Epistle to the Corinthians,* Philip E. Hughes, 284.
2. Tim Hansel, *You Gotta Keep Dancing* (Life Journey Books, Elgin, Illinois, 1985), 41.

Chapter Eight

1. The issues that many scholars raise because of the change in the tone of chapter 10 are, *Was this section a part of 2 Corinthians originally? Was it a later edition? Or was it even written by Paul?* Significant changes in thought in biblical documents have been seen by liberal theologians and scholars as an opportunity to attack the reliability and credibility of the Bible. We, who believe that the Bible is the word of God and a product of God's inspiration, accept that the individual letters and books which make up the Bible are authentic and are actually written by men who were inspired to do so. In order for the Bible to be denied, it has to be shown to be a forgery, or in other words, that it was written by someone who was neither an actual apostle nor inspired.

   One of the ways that liberal scholars attempt to prove the Bible's fallibility is to question the various sections of a letter or book and ask whether the sections were truly written by the same author. Chapter 10 of 2 Corinthians gives them an opportunity to seriously ask if this section—because of its change in tone and content—was part of the original letter, or whether it was later added by someone else.

   Whereas it has always been my conviction that God gives everyone the right to ask questions (asking questions is essential in the search for the truth), asking questions can be a ploy to evade the truth. Anybody can ask a question. It takes very little intelligence to do that—following through and finding answers is the challenge. The reason I am bringing all of this up is because of the prevalence of these discussions in many Bible commentaries on the market today.

A change in tone or theme is not that unusual in documents of substantial length. It is highly unlikely that Paul wrote the whole letter to the Corinthians (or to the Romans) in one sitting. For him to change his tone or to switch gears in thought is normal. It is quite possible that an expert in literary style could examine this commentary and notice the same thing. However, it is still all mine. New thoughts and emotions, along with having to take breaks in writing, all contribute to a difference in style, word choice and emphasis. There are times when I write with a lot of energy, while at other times I am extremely tired, and even a bit bored, yet it is still all my work nonetheless. The bottom line is that all of the manuscripts that we have of 2 Corinthians have Paul listing himself as its author. Other theories up to this point are purely speculative.

Practical Exposition Series

Life to the Full
A study of the writings of James, Peter, John and Jude
by Douglas Jacoby

Mine Eyes Have Seen the Glory
The victory of the Lamb in the Book of Revelation
by Gordon Ferguson

Power in Weakness
Second Corinthians and the Ministry of Paul
by Marty Wooten

The Daily Power Series
Series Editors: Thomas and Sheila Jones

Thirty Days at the Foot of the Cross
A study of the central issue of Christianity

First...the Kingdom
A study of the Sermon on the Mount

The Mission
The inspiring task of the church in every generation

Teach Us to Pray
A study of the most vital of all spiritual disciplines

To Live Is Christ
An interactive study of the Letter to the Philippians

Glory in the Church
God's plan to shine through his church

The Victory of Surrender
An in-depth study of a powerful biblical concept
(workbook and tapes also available)
by Gordon Ferguson

The Fine Art of Hospitality
edited by Sheila Jones
The Fine Art of Hospitality Handbook
edited by Sheila Jones and Betty Dyson
(two-volume set)

True and Reasonable
Evidences for God in a skeptical world
by Douglas Jacoby

Raising Awesome Kids in Troubled Times
by Sam and Geri Laing

Let It Shine: A Devotional Book for Teens
edited by Thomas and Sheila Jones

Mind Change: The Overcomer's Handbook
by Thomas A. Jones

She Shall Be Called Woman
Volume I: Old Testament Women
edited by Sheila Jones and Linda Brumley

She Shall Be Called Woman
Volume II: New Testament Women
edited by Sheila Jones and Linda Brumley

For information about ordering these
and many other resources from DPI, call
1-800-727-8273
or from outside the U.S.
617-938-7396
or write to
DPI, One Merrill Street, Woburn, MA 01801-4629